LEVERAGE

Praise for *Leverage*

"God's word is clear; you can serve God or money but
not both. Ken Boa and Russ Crosson are two of the most
qualified people I know who can speak to this issue with
wisdom and experience. I recommend this book highly."

RON BLUE, FOUNDER OF KINGDOM ADVISORS

"Generosity is one of the four core values of the Batterson
family, along with humility, gratitude, and courage. I'm
grateful for Ken Boa and Russ Crosson writing this book that
provides very practical ways of living and giving generously."

MARK BATTERSON, *NEW YORK TIMES* BESTSELLING AUTHOR OF
THE CIRCLE MAKER; LEAD PASTOR OF NATIONAL COMMUNITY CHURCH

"Many aspire to be generous—when they're older, wealthier, or
more established—but whatever our phase of life, generosity begins
now in the way we steward our time, talent, and treasure. As we
grow in generosity, we will undoubtedly find that what is good
for the world around us is also good for our soul. I'm grateful
for the dynamic partnership between theologian Ken Boa and
practitioner Russ Crosson—and their impactful new book Leverage
that will undoubtedly help us grow into greater generosity."

PETER GREER, PRESIDENT AND CEO OF HOPE
INTERNATIONAL; COAUTHOR OF *MISSION DRIFT*

LEVERAGE

Using Temporal Wealth for Eternal Gain

Kenneth Boa and Russ Crosson

 TRINITY HOUSE PUBLISHERS

One Piedmont Center, Suite 130, Atlanta, Georgia 30305.
(800) DRAW NEAR (372-9632). trinityhousepublishers.org.

Cover art by Stephen Crotts.
Interior design by Victoria Corish.

Contents

Preface

Russ Crosson

It was a late fall afternoon when the phone rang in my office. I recognized the voice on the other end immediately. It was the son of a long-time client of mine who I knew had been in declining health. "Dad has gone home to be with the Lord," the son said. Although I knew it was coming, it was still difficult to accept. I sat down, composed myself, and offered my condolences to the family.

A few days later, my wife, Julie, and I traveled to the funeral in the small town where this gentleman had lived and worked for more than six decades. On the drive, we reminisced about the impact he had had on our growing family over the years. He and his wife were like second grandparents to our sons and always made us feel loved and welcomed whenever we were with them. We had mentally prepared for this day, but it still seemed surreal that he was actually gone from this earth. My wife and I had made this drive every year for the past thirty years, but this time it was different. I could not help but think that a day like this is in each of our futures.

We arrived about twenty minutes before the service was scheduled to begin and were surprised to realize there was no parking left. Fortunately, I saw the son, who escorted us to a special parking place. As we were ushered into the church, I looked around and realized it was standing room only. All the seats were filled, and there were several rows of people standing around the sides and back of the sanctuary. It seemed like the whole town was in attendance.

During the service, the son took the podium. As he made comments about his dad, he began asking for audience participation. He articulated all the ways his dad had exhibited generosity in this small town and asked those who had experienced it to stand. Before I knew it, everyone in the building was standing. As I looked around, I realized that is what I want my funeral to look like—people impacted because I leveraged my temporal wealth for something beyond myself. I want people to remember me for living a generous life and investing in others.

As Julie and I drove home that night, we reflected on what we had witnessed. For more than thirty-five years, we had watched this man and his family embody the concept of living generously and leveraging temporal wealth for eternal impact. He did not start off being generous. However, he grew to understand and embrace the principles and practices that we will share in this book. He chose to open his hands and bless others with God's financial blessings to him.

The visual of the people standing and giving their testimonies of his impact at the funeral was imprinted in our minds. He had left a mark on the people who came after him, and hundreds of them had filled the church to pay tribute and honor to him. People endure. Material things don't. This truth was vivid in my mind as I reflected on what I had just experienced and contrasted it to a book I had recently read about a wealthy British sea merchant named Godfrey Barnsley.[1]

There is an exquisite vacation destination north of Atlanta, Georgia, called Barnsley Resort. My wife and I have enjoyed some time there over the years. During one of our visits, I picked up a book that told the history of the resort and gardens. The story fascinated me. Godfrey Barnsley was one of the wealthiest men in the world in the early 1800s. He directed a shipping empire that sailed the world's seas and transported 60 percent of the South's cotton to his native England and to other markets. He was well respected all over the world.

Barnsley decided to build a luxurious and magnificent home for his wife, Julia. He purchased four thousand acres of land in the

---

1   Clent Coker, *Barnsley Gardens at Woodland* (The Julia Publishing Company, 2000).

wilderness of northwest Georgia and created a vast estate and gardens. Since his wealth was so immense, he shipped in hundreds of rare trees and shrubs—ancient cedars from Lebanon and other bushes from around the world. He chose handcrafted windows with sterling silver latches, marble from Italy and France, and priceless furnishings from the four corners of the world. It was one of the most exquisite antebellum estates east of the Mississippi River. Unfortunately, his wife passed away before the home was completed in 1848, but several generations of the family lived at the estate until 1942. However, by the 1980s, the home and grounds were vacant and falling into ruins. In 1988, the property was purchased by an investor who developed it into the upscale resort it is today. If you go to Barnsley Resort, all that remains of Godfrey Barnsley's investment is a pile of rocks known as the "Manor House Ruins."

When your time on earth is finished, which legacy would you prefer: a sanctuary full of people impacted by how you lived your life and utilized your money, or a mound of rocks? We must choose whether we are going to invest in the *here and now* (our temporal home) or in the *there and future* (our eternal home). Leveraging our resources according to what God says, such as by investing in people, will last; investing in buildings and temporal goods, such as Barnsley's estate, will not.

The first-century apostles understood this choice. They did not invest in things of this world (we don't go to work in the Peter Pavilion or the Pauline Plaza), but rather they invested in people by proclaiming the gospel. You and I enjoy great gain as a result of their focus on eternal things, and we are called to continue that purpose and leverage our wealth for the benefit of others to the glory of God.

Introduction

Kenneth Boa and Russ Crosson

A lever is a simple machine that increases efficiency by amplifying a small force and turning it into a much larger one, opening up a realm of mechanical possibilities. As the Greek mathematician Archimedes famously said, "Give me a lever long enough and a fulcrum on which to place it, and I shall move the world."

While Archimedes's scope focused solely on the material and the finite, this book applies the principle of leverage to matters of infinite importance. Whether or not we realize it, we use the principle of leverage on a daily basis, not simply in physics but in the sense of turning limited resources into an advantage—often a selfish advantage that gives us gain at the expense of other people. Although the link between leverage and selfish gain is so well forged that the two may seem synonymous, this book seeks to show how Christians can leverage God's earthly gifts not for personal benefit but for the advancement of His kingdom.

In Scripture, we see that biblical wisdom is skill in the art of living, which involves treating things according to their true value. We all have two choices: we can follow the wisdom of the world, or we can follow the wisdom of God. Following the wisdom of the world is folly, but it is the route we take by default. The world clamors for our attention and encourages us to find our identity in what is temporal rather than in what is eternal. Earthly wisdom peddles a false sense of control and security, consistently encouraging us to accumulate for ourselves the seven Ps of idolatry: possessions, pleasure, prestige, popularity, promotion, power, and performance. When these temporal things pass away, they will not leave us with any eternal gain. To pursue them is folly.

Following the wisdom of God, on the other hand, requires training and discipline. As we spend time in Scripture and come to know and love God more, the wisdom of the world will have less of a hold on us. Instead of seeking control by hoarding material wealth on earth, we can relinquish our attempt at autonomy and recognize that we are stewards of what God has given us. Biblical wisdom urges us to transmute what we are given in our visible, temporal world into treasures of the invisible, eternal world (Matthew 6:19–20). Life, after all, does not consist in the abundance of our possessions, but in being rich toward God, using our earthly riches to honor Him (Luke 12:15, 21).

Living with the end in mind is the key to stewarding God's gifts well and leveraging them for His kingdom. For Christians, this earthbound life is a prelude to an eternity in heaven, but our sight is often fixed on our earthly horizon. We fail to apprehend the "city that has foundations, whose designer and builder is God" (Hebrews 11:10). Never having been there and experienced that city, we have no memories of it, and so we live as if this earth were our final home.

But biblical wisdom reorients us, inviting us to use our resources wisely by investing in our relationships and in the Word of God as we follow Jesus.

God has provided each of us with a certain amount of time, talent, and treasure to leverage for His kingdom work in our unique sphere of influence. At the *bēma*, the judgment seat of Christ, God will reveal if we used those resources wisely for His glory (1 Corinthians 4:1–5; 2 Corinthians 5:10).

In this book, we will focus on how to leverage our monetary resources for God's eternal kingdom. Chances are, if you are reading this book, you are rich—but what does that mean? As soon as we try to define "rich," we run into the problem of comparison. We usually compare the resources of those who have more than we do with our own resources, thinking of *them* as rich and *us* as not rich. The truth is, though, that if you have clean water, food, shelter, clothing, opportunities for jobs, and transportation—even if that transportation is public—then you have an abundance of resources compared to billions of people around the world. Anything more than these basic needs, and you are rich.

Especially in the Western world, this is not how we like to think of being "rich." A six-figure income, a tidy sum for our retirement account, our dream house, a fancy car—these are goals we often strive for and take for granted. We usually do not consider ourselves rich even if we achieve them, and certainly not *before* we reach them.

The problem with this mindset is that we think we need to amass more and more wealth to be "rich." And often, the more wealth we have, the harder it is to be generous and leverage our finances for God's kingdom work (Ecclesiastes 5:10). One reason for this difficulty is that the more we accumulate, the more tempted we are to find our security and satisfaction in our bank account, not realizing that God has blessed us so we can bless others.

Like Paul, we want to challenge you to reevaluate your financial situation and ask the Holy Spirit to guide you into greater generosity, laying up lasting treasures:

Instruct those who are rich in this present world not to be conceited or to fix their hope on the uncertainty of riches, but on God, who richly supplies us with all things to enjoy. Instruct them to do good, to be rich in good works, to be generous and ready to share, storing up for themselves the treasure of a good foundation for the future, so that they may take hold of that which is life indeed.

(1 Timothy 6:17–19 NASB)

Financial prosperity, while lauded by the world, lends itself to earthly-mindedness if we are not careful, particularly when we treat our wealth with a sense of entitlement rather than recognizing that God entrusted it to us. Because material wealth will not survive beyond this earthly life, biblical wisdom invites us to grasp our finiteness and spurs us to live with a pilgrim mindset, investing our resources in what is to come through our good works and generosity.

How to Use This Book

The goal of this book is to help you learn how to leverage the resources God has given you for His kingdom. It contains two parts, combining the wisdom of a biblical scholar and a financial expert:

- **Part One: Principles of Biblical Leverage**
- **Part Two: Practices of Biblical Leverage**

Part One, written primarily by Kenneth Boa, guides you through the *principles* of biblical generosity, addressing the *why*, the *when*, the *how*, the *how much*, and the *where* of giving. Because you first have to know what biblical generosity looks like in order to put it into practice, Part One provides the groundwork for the practical applications in Part Two.

Part Two, written primarily by Russ Crosson, moves from the biblical principles of generosity to practical financial applications that will aid you in your endeavors to give more generously. These practices will help you manage your financial resources according to biblical wisdom in a way that leverages them for greater generosity and, subsequently, eternal gain.

The principles we give in Part One apply to all of us, no matter the size of our income. God, after all, can take the smallest of gifts and multiply it (Matthew 14:13–21), and when we give generously (even if we are only able to give a small amount), He is pleased (Luke 21:1–4). At the same time, we specifically want to challenge the wealthy to increase their generosity, recognizing that it is a peculiar fact that the more wealth we have, the stingier we often become.

Our prayer is that you will order your lives and leverage your resources so that you can say with confidence at the end of your days, "I have fought the good fight, I have finished the race, I have kept the faith. Henceforth there is laid up for me the crown of righteousness" (2 Timothy 4:7–8a).

PART ONE:

Principles of
Biblical Leverage

KENNETH BOA

Before we can treat material wealth according to its true value, we first have to orient our lives according to biblical principles. Without biblical wisdom, we will fall into folly, which is the way of the world. The axiom that anything left to itself will move into increased disorder is especially true of spiritual matters. Whereas the world defines us by default, the Word defines us by discipline. This is possible only through the continuous renewal of our minds with spiritual truths.

We find these spiritual truths in Scripture, but merely knowing them is not enough. We must reinforce belief with behavior, or we will find that we are investing in the world rather than in the Word. Here's a quick test: What do you spend your time and money on? As it has often been said, your calendar and your checkbook (or mobile banking record) are good indicators of your objects of pursuit. We may *say* we are seeking God's kingdom first, but our daily rhythms reveal our true priorities. Often, our habits reveal that we serve money as our master (Matthew 6:24), making it necessary for us to renew our minds over and over again in spiritual truths.

As we search Scripture, we find that we are accountable to our Creator for the things He has entrusted to us. This realization should be a powerful motivator for us to leverage all that we have for His glory. After all, everything we own really belongs to God, and He gives us the resources we have to meet our needs (Philippians 4:19). He may provide an abundance for us in a season so that we can meet the needs of others, or He may allow us to experience lack, often so that we might benefit from the generosity of a fellow Christian.

The Bible makes it clear that Christians are not promised material wealth; neither financial abundance nor the lack thereof is an indication of an individual's faithfulness. On the contrary, God uses financial abundance as a tool to refine and reveal our faithfulness. What counts is what we do with the resources He has entrusted us with. If we find ourselves with an abundance—whether great or small—God calls us to serve and glorify Him with it through our generosity.

On the whole, the more money we have, the easier it is to find our identity in it. For this reason, Paul warns against making an idol of riches.

> For we brought nothing into the world, and we cannot take anything out of the world. But if we have food and clothing, with these we will be content. But those who desire to be rich fall into temptation, into a snare, into many senseless and harmful desires that plunge people into ruin and destruction. For the love of money is a root of all kinds of evils. It is through this craving that some have wandered away from the faith and pierced themselves with many pangs.
>
> (1 Timothy 6:7–10)

How do we heed Paul's warning and prevent a love of money from distancing us from God? It starts by answering the following questions with biblical principles:

- Why are we to give?
- When are we to give?
- How are we to give?
- How much are we to give?
- Where are we to give?

The principles in Part One will aid you in understanding the reason for generosity, and we hope they will encourage you in your own journey of trusting God with your resources.

CHAPTER 1

Why Are We to Give?

In the early 1970s, when I was a seminary student learning how to convey the gospel to the unreached, money was very tight. There were a number of times when my wife, Karen, and I weren't sure how we were going to pay the bills. On each of these occasions, monetary gifts unexpectedly appeared in my mailbox in exactly the amount that we needed to get by. What was significant about these gifts—and the reason why I still recall them vividly half a century later—was not their amount but the fact that their givers had chosen to respond faithfully to the Spirit's prompting. Through these acts of faith, my young family experienced God's provision of both material sustenance and spiritual encouragement. This is ultimately why God calls Christians to give: to participate in God's kingdom work by providing for the needs of fellow believers and demonstrating His love to others through generosity.

An Invitation to Participate in Kingdom Work

Generosity toward God's people stems from a biblically correct understanding of the role of money in our lives. Jesus frequently used money to demonstrate spiritual truths in His parables because money so clearly illustrates the temporal versus the eternal (see Matthew 13:44–46; 25:14–30 as examples). The currency of that which is passing away is measured by metrics of the visible, palpable, and quantifiable—metrics that are familiar and comfortable to us on this side of heaven. On the other hand, the currency of the kingdom of God is built on the only two things present in this earthly world that will endure: the Word of God and relationships. To see money as separate from this kingdom currency is to create a false dichotomy between the sacred and the secular. When we live with Christ at the center of our lives, it follows that every aspect of our lives can be used for His glory. Wealth is no exception. Although it is a visible currency of this world, God calls us to leverage this temporal resource (like all our resources) for His kingdom, investing it in our relationships and in the spread of the gospel.

Make no mistake about it: the purpose of money is to provide for needs—for our own, yes, but especially for those of other people. Instead of storing up wealth for our own satisfaction, God calls us to share generously with others, investing in our relationships. This is not because He needs our wealth in order to bless others. Scripture is replete with the truth that the Lord of creation does not need our wealth (see Psalm 104), and that His purposes will not be thwarted by those who choose not to give what is His in the first place. But the Bible also teaches that although we cannot contribute anything to God since He has no needs, He offers us the dignity of participation in His purposes. We see this principle in Philippians 4:15–19:

> And you Philippians yourselves know that in the beginning of the gospel, when I left Macedonia, no church entered into partnership with me in giving and receiving, except you only. Even in Thessalonica you sent me help for my needs once and again. Not that I seek the gift, but I seek the fruit that increases to your credit. I have received full payment, and more. I am well supplied, having received from Epaphroditus the gifts you sent, a fragrant offering, a sacrifice acceptable and pleasing to God. And my God will supply every need of yours according to his riches in glory in Christ Jesus.

God could have provided for Paul without the Philippians' help, but He gave them wealth as an opportunity to increase the fruit of their faith. Paul rejoices in the fact that they chose to give generously and bless him financially in response to this opportunity.

God gives us wealth in order to present us with such opportunities, while He withholds wealth from others as a chance to manifest His glory and strengthen the fellowship of believers. Paul demonstrates this in 2 Corinthians 8:13–15, explaining how the apparent imbalance in God's distribution of material wealth among believers is an invitation to participate in meeting the needs of others:

> For I do not mean that others should be eased and you burdened, *but that as a matter of fairness your abundance at the present time should supply their need, so that their abundance may supply your need, that there may be fairness.* As it is written, "Whoever gathered much had nothing left over, and whoever gathered little had no lack."[2]

---

2   Emphasis added.

God does not give wealth equally to all people, but He expects us to share what we are able with one another. We participate in His kingdom work when we give out of our abundance, and we also benefit from His kingdom work when we receive resources from others in our times of need. Times of abundance and times of lack are both opportunities for spiritual growth and the increase of our trust in God.

Having an abundance of wealth is an invitation to have an abundance of generosity. Our temptation is to store up wealth to meet our perceived needs, to provide security for every potential financial crisis, and to enjoy "the good life," but that is not why God gives us riches. Before we spend money on a second house (or a third, fourth, or fifth house), extra cars, numerous expensive vacations, or any other luxury, we need to examine the motives of our heart (Jeremiah 22:13–14; Haggai 1:4). Are we giving everything God is calling us to give, or is it possible that we are losing sight of eternal riches by storing up wealth for ourselves on earth? Have we asked God His will for our material goods and submitted to His plans for us? Are we cultivating a heart that tends toward generosity, obedience, and trust in God?

As we answer these questions and prayerfully surrender our material goods to God, we need to be careful of our motives. "The heart," after all, "is deceitful above all things, and desperately sick; who can understand it?" (Jeremiah 17:9). Our inherent tendency is toward selfishness. It is easy to excuse our excess when we would do better to give our wealth away. Seeking an accountability partner—someone with whom we share our financial situation and ask to hold us accountable for how we spend our wealth—can provide a safeguard against these selfish tendencies to accumulate wealth (see chapter 6). Ultimately, though, only the work of the Holy Spirit in our hearts enables us to give generously, which is why we must take care to submit our finances to Him regularly, especially if our wealth increases.

At the same time, having only a little wealth is not an excuse to withhold our resources from others and become stingy.

In 2 Corinthians 8:1–5, Paul praises the Macedonians for giving out of what little they had to their impoverished brothers and sisters in Jerusalem:

> We want you to know, brothers, about the grace of God that has been given among the churches of Macedonia, for in a severe test of affliction, their abundance of joy and their extreme poverty have overflowed in a wealth of generosity on their part. For they gave according to their means, as I can testify, and beyond their means, of their own accord, begging us earnestly for the favor of taking part in the relief of the saints— and this, not as we expected, but they gave themselves first to the Lord and then by the will of God to us.

The kingdom mindset of generosity we see in this passage stems from having a relationship with Christ. Instead of clinging to their earthly wealth, the saints in Macedonia "begged earnestly" to give because they had first surrendered themselves to God and were following the example of Christ. This is why Paul draws a parallel between the Macedonians' financial generosity and the paragon of humility and sacrifice embodied in Jesus Christ: "For you know the grace of our Lord Jesus Christ, that though he was rich, yet for your sake he became poor, so that you by his poverty might become rich" (2 Corinthians 8:9). There is no greater generosity than Christ's sacrifice of Himself for our sake. The more we understand and give thanks for what He has done for us, the less hold money will have on our lives. Like Christ, we are to give of our resources and bless others through our generosity, responding to God's invitation to participate in His kingdom work.

Six Reasons for Giving

God's greatest desire is for us to give ourselves wholly and unreservedly to Him, and a palpable expression of that is how we leverage our temporal possessions for His kingdom. Spirit-led generosity enables us to define ourselves more and more by who and whose we are and less and less by our earthly portfolio. The following list gives six reasons why we ought to accept God's invitation to participate in His kingdom work of generous giving. [3]

1. Giving is a tangible way to acknowledge the ultimate *ownership* and *provision* of the sovereign God in our lives (Deuteronomy 8:11–19; Psalm 24:1; 50:10–12; Haggai 2:8; 1 Corinthians 4:7; 2 Corinthians 9:8).

As mentioned earlier in this chapter, God does not need us to give—He already owns everything. However, He does invite us to participate in His kingdom work through giving. When we do so, we express our trust in His provision, acknowledging that all things come from His hand. Seeking to store up wealth for ourselves is fruitless; God gave it to us, and He can take it away (Job 1:21). He can also multiply it, blessing us abundantly as we generously give to others.

The example of the Israelites wandering in the wilderness demonstrates the faithfulness of God to provide for His people. God met their material needs for forty years through the miracles of daily food (manna and quail), clothing that did not wear out, and physical fortitude (Deuteronomy 8:3–4). The same God who provided for the Israelites continues to exercise full authority over our material provisions today. As He did then, He calls us to trust in Him and avoid the arrogant autonomy of trusting in our own hand through the accumulation of wealth.

2. We show *honor* and *obedience* to God in our giving because God commands us to give (Proverbs 3:9–10; Matthew 6:19–21; 25:31–46; Luke 6:38; 12:33; 1 Timothy 6:17–19).

When we give generously, we put our faith into action through obedience, honoring God with the resources He has entrusted to us and becoming more *theocentric* (God-centered) instead of *egocentric* (self-centered).

---

3   List adapted from the Ronald Blue Trust training manual.

The Gospels provide warnings against self-driven (versus king-dom-driven) wealth management:

> Do not lay up for yourselves treasures on earth, where moth and rust destroy and where thieves break in and steal, but lay up for yourselves treasures in heaven, where neither moth nor rust destroys and where thieves do not break in and steal. For where your treasure is, there your heart will be also.

> (Matthew 6:19–21)

> Sell your possessions, and give to the needy. Provide yourselves with moneybags that do not grow old, with a treasure in the heavens that does not fail, where no thief approaches and no moth destroys.

> (Luke 12:33)

It is foolish to store up treasures on earth because our time here is fleeting and uncertain. By contrast, treasure in heaven is "an inheritance that is imperishable, undefiled, and unfading" (1 Peter 1:4). When we value God, we will obey Him and honor Him with our financial resources, giving up earthly gain for our eternal inheritance in Christ—even at great material cost to ourselves.

3. Giving is a tangible way to *worship* and show *gratitude* to God (Matthew 6:21; Mark 14:3–9; Romans 12:1–2; 2 Corinthians 8:1–6).

Giving is a form of worship, which is the commitment and consecration of ourselves to God. Generous giving shows that we are not putting our hope in temporal goods but in God, giving thanks to Him for who He is and how He has cared for us. This type of worship was especially clear in the old covenant sacrificial system. Three times a year, the Israelites were required to go to the tabernacle or temple and bring the best of their produce/livestock to worship and show gratitude to God (see Deuteronomy 26).

Although we are no longer under the old covenant, our gratitude should be even stronger now that Christ has completed His work on the cross and given us the free gift of salvation in Him. We sacrifice our material wealth to Him and do good works to the praise of His glorious grace out of gratitude for the love He has lavished on us (Ephesians 1:3–10).

4. Giving *breaks the power of money* and helps us *prioritize the issues of life* (Proverbs 18:10–11; Mark 10:17–31; Luke 12:33–34; 16:11–13; 1 Timothy 6:9–10).

If making God central in our attitude toward our finances draws us closer to Him through obedience and worship, failing to center our lives on God makes us vulnerable to spiritual snares. First Timothy 6:9 makes this clear: "Those who desire to be rich fall into temptation, into a snare, into many senseless and harmful desires that plunge people into ruin and destruction." Wealth has a downward pull; it is not neutral any more than sex and power are. It tempts us to find our security and identity in it.

Arrogance can lead to the deadly supposition that it was our hand, not God's, that brought us financial security. Greed steadily inflates our answer to the question, "How much is enough?" while simultaneously diminishing our ability to live by faith. We then forget God's calling to participate in His kingdom work through generous giving, looking instead to wealth to satisfy us. This results in a tragic irony, as we cannot be satiated if we fix our hope on worldly things and forget the ultimate source of our wealth. In truth, no earthbound good or felicity can satisfy the aspirations of the human heart. The freight of human aspiration is so great that only eternity can sustain it.

5. Charitable giving is done to *meet the needs* of others (Exodus 16:18; Leviticus 23:22; Deuteronomy 15:10–11; 2 Corinthians 9:12–14; Philippians 4:16; 1 John 3:17).

In both the Old and the New Testament, we read of God's call to provide for the needs of others through generous giving. In the Old

Testament, God commanded His people to leave the gleanings of the fields for the poor to gather. These gleanings might otherwise have increased the landowners' profits by as much as 10 percent, so it can be seen as a sort of "passive tithe"—a method of giving generously by providing work and food for anyone in need instead of hoarding resources out of greed (Leviticus 23:22).

Although we do not have the same passive tithe as the Israelites, God still calls us to provide for those in need. When it comes to managing money, we are to follow Jesus' precedent in exchanging our good for the good of others. In practice, the first step is often to share what we are given with our closest connections—our family members—in order to build a legacy of strong relationships and meet their needs. First Timothy 5:8 tells us, "But if anyone does not provide for his relatives, and especially for members of his household, he has denied the faith and is worse than an unbeliever." And if we imagine our lives as concentric circles of influence, once we have provided for our families (the core), we can expand our giving by moving outward to subsequent rings. These outer circles include friends who are in need, members of our church, and other ministries to which the Spirit guides us (see chapter 5 for more on where to give).

6. We draw spiritual *rewards* from the act of giving (Matthew 6:20; 16:27; Luke 12:33; Romans 2:6–11; 1 Corinthians 3:8–15; 2 Corinthians 5:10; Philippians 4:17; Revelation 22:12).

Although salvation is by grace through faith in Christ, we still receive rewards for our faithfulness to His calling. We read in 1 Corinthians 3:11, "No one can lay a foundation other than that which is laid, which is Jesus Christ," but we are still called to build on that foundation through our good works in the power of the Holy Spirit. The ideas of grace and reward may seem contradictory, but Scripture tells us that these good works and rewards are God's gift to us in the first place (2 Corinthians 8:1; Ephesians 2:10). God graciously grants us the ability to respond to His call and rewards us when we accept His invitation to participate in His kingdom work.

As we consider the principle of receiving rewards in heaven, we need to be careful to avoid projecting the world's values into heaven. There is not a one-to-one correspondence regarding what we give up on earth and what we gain in heaven. For example, if we give fifty dollars here, we will not receive fifty dollars up there, because earthly currency is different than heavenly currency. We will gain spiritual reward,[4] increasing our capacity to know God and reflect His glory, as well as increasing our capacity for community.[5] It is also important to note that, although we will receive varying levels of reward in heaven (Matthew 25:14–30; 1 Corinthians 3:10–15), no one will be unhappy in heaven. Our joy will be complete in the presence of the glory of God, and our rewards serve to magnify not ourselves, but the glory of God (Revelation 4:10–11).[6]

The next few chapters outline how, on a practical level, we can leverage that which is passing away into the currency of that which will last forever. By seeking daily a "heart of wisdom" (Psalm 90:12) and following the Spirit's leading on the specifics of giving (when, how, how much, and where), we can boldly reflect the extravagant blessing and encouragement God has offered to us, time and time again, and to His other image-bearers.

---

4   We may also gain earthly reward, such as through the benefits of tax deductibility on charitable giving. However, our eyes should be fixed on the eternal rather than the temporal. Tax deduction in itself is not a reason to give, although it is an earthly benefit.

5   For more on this topic, see Kenneth Boa, "Motivated Spirituality: Love, Gratitude, and Rewards," in *Conformed to His Image: Biblical, Practical Approaches to Spiritual Formation*, rev. ed. (Grand Rapids, MI: Zondervan Academic, 2020), 132–137.

6   For this reason, we will also not have envy of others in heaven. Instead, we will rejoice in their greater reward, so that each of us will experience a fullness of joy and satisfaction in Christ. For further reading, see Jonathan Edwards's sermon on Romans 2:10, which can be accessed online for free at www.ccel.org/ccel/edwards/works2.xv.viii.html.

CHAPTER 2

When Are We to Give?

God provides for us not once, not twice, but a multitude of times throughout our lives. Consider all that He gives: the basics of food, water, clothing,
and shelter; relationships; the complex wonders of the natural world;
the joy of music; the aesthetic beauty of art—the list could go on and
on. When we examine the blessings in our lives, it becomes clear that
God gives generously to us on a consistent basis. Everything in life is gift
and grace. Recognizing this truth enables us to imitate our Creator and
leverage our temporal wealth for eternal gain by making the profoundly
countercultural choice to give of our resources consistently during our
lifetime and to listen to the Holy Spirit's promptings.

Give Consistently

When it comes to the biblical principles of giving, the first thing that probably comes to mind is the Old Testament practice of tithing. These commandments to tithe no longer apply to the believer under the new covenant, but we can still draw insights about God's desire for generosity from the principles behind the commandments.

Most people assume there was a single 10 percent tithe in the Old Testament. However, there are actually three active tithes mentioned in the Old Testament, as well as a passive tithe, in addition to numerous freewill offerings. Consistent, generous giving was an integral part of the Old Testament sacrificial system.

The first tithe in the Old Testament is the Levitical tithe, a 10 percent tithe of produce and animals that the Israelites gave to the Levites (Numbers 18:21, 24). They did so because the Levites did not have a livelihood or an inheritance. Instead, they dedicated their time to the service of the tabernacle/temple as God's priestly tribe. The tithe was their means of support so that they could continue to lead the Israelites in worship.

Second, the Israelites worshiped the Lord through the tithe of the feasts (Deuteronomy 14:22–27). For this tithe, the people took 10 percent of their firstfruits and the firstborn of their animals and celebrated in a festival before the Lord in the tabernacle/temple. If the distance they had to travel was too far for the food to remain fresh, then they sold the produce, took the profit with them, and purchased whatever they wanted in order to celebrate before the Lord. This personal tithe demonstrated their dedication to God; instead of hoarding their resources, they honored God by celebrating Him lavishly in worship.

The third active tithe in the Old Testament is the poor tithe (Deuteronomy 14:28–29), which occurred once every three years. It mandated that the Israelites care for the widows, orphans, and sojourners in their land by providing for their needs.

Furthermore, as mentioned in chapter 1, there was a passive tithe. God commanded the Israelites not to reap all the produce from their harvests (Leviticus 23:22), but to leave the gleanings for the poor of the land. This could have amounted to as much as 10 percent of their potential profit.

These four tithes were practiced on a consistent basis—two occurred once every year, the third every three years, and the fourth whenever there was a harvest. Although we do not have the same commands to tithe in the New Testament, because our economy is no longer based on agriculture and because we are no longer under the Mosaic Law, the principle of consistent giving remains the same. Instead of hoarding our possessions, God commands us to give freely.

Consider Paul's directions for consistent giving in 1 Corinthians 16:1–2:

> Now concerning the collection for the saints: as I directed the churches of Galatia, so you also are to do. *On the first day of every week*, each of you is to put something aside and store it up, as he may prosper, so that there will be no collecting when I come.[7]

This passage refers to a singular giving event—a collection for the church in Jerusalem—but the principle here is key. Paul told the churches in Galatia as well as the Corinthians to set aside some of their resources on a weekly basis. He did not set an amount, but it is clear that he expected the churches to give a portion of their income whenever they "prospered." In modern practice, this could look like setting aside a regular portion of our paycheck to give away. It could also mean setting an amount to give regularly based on our net worth, depending on our income level (we'll look into this practice in chapter 8).

Paul further commends consistent giving in Philippians 4:15–18:

> And you Philippians yourselves know that in the beginning of the gospel, when I left Macedonia, no church entered into partnership with me in giving and receiving,

---

7   Emphasis added.

except you only. Even in Thessalonica you sent me help for my needs once and again. Not that I seek the gift, but I seek the fruit that increases to your credit. I have received full payment, and more. I am well supplied, having received from Epaphroditus the gifts you sent, a fragrant offering, a sacrifice acceptable and pleasing to God.

The Philippian church supported Paul financially in his ministry of spreading the gospel. Paul describes their giving as a "partnership," implying a commitment to regularly give and provide for his needs. This regular commitment benefitted both Paul and the Philippians.

First, a commitment to give regularly benefitted Paul. As a missionary, he was able to receive steady support as he preached the gospel, enabling him more security in his work. Now, Paul did not always take gifts from the people he served, avoiding the potential accusation that he was idly taking money and getting rich like other false teachers (1 Corinthians 9:15–18). However, he does commend the practice of giving consistently so that those who proclaim the gospel can "get their living by the gospel" (1 Corinthians 9:14). His commendation stems from the principle behind the Levitical tithe in the Old Testament. Just as the consistent giving of the Israelites allowed the Levites to continue to serve in the temple, so our consistent giving enables pastors and missionaries to continue to preach the gospel (1 Corinthians 9:13).

Second, consistent giving also benefitted the Philippian believers. By supporting Paul on a consistent basis, the Philippian believers increased their "fruit"—they experienced spiritual growth as a result of their giving. Likewise today, the practice of regular disbursements is a discipline that allows us to steward our kingdom resources well, particularly if our income or net worth increases. Of course, we can and should make one-time gifts as the Spirit leads us, but giving regularly is a safeguard against storing up earthly wealth. Not only will we be able to provide stable support to organizations and individuals, but we will also avoid hoarding temporal treasure and store up treasure in heaven.

Consistent giving requires a kingdom mindset, in which our own benefit (using our wealth for ourselves) is outweighed by what is beneficial to others (generously giving our resources to those in need). At the end of the day, life is not about acquisition; it is about investing in the lives of eternal beings. This understanding makes an enormous difference in our decision-making, for when we see giving as an opportunity to serve and to bless other people, we will desire to do so consistently. The more we give away our money, the easier it becomes to do so, spring-loading us toward giving rather than hoarding.

Give Now, Not Later

Not only does Scripture demonstrate the principle of consistent giving, but it also exhorts us to give during this lifetime instead of merely at the end of our life in our will or in a foundation. This is the practice of giving with a warm (living) hand rather than a cold (dead) hand, otherwise known as current versus deferred giving (see chapter 7).

God hates hoarding and loves lavish generosity—particularly in the context of investing in our relationships. However, many believers choose to give with a cold hand rather than with a warm hand, giving only when they no longer have a use for their stores of wealth. While leaving assets to meet needs through a will is not wrong—indeed, it is wise to write our wishes down for how our resources ought to be distributed when we die—the Bible does not condone hoarding wealth during this life.

We see this principle in the parable of the rich fool in Luke 12:16–21.

> And [Jesus] told them a parable, saying, "The land of
> a rich man produced plentifully, and he thought to
> himself, 'What shall I do, for I have nowhere to store
> my crops?' And he said, 'I will do this: I will tear down
> my barns and build larger ones, and there I will store
> all my grain and my goods. And I will say to my soul,
> "Soul, you have ample goods laid up for many years;

relax, eat, drink, be merry."' But God said to him,
'Fool! This night your soul is required of you, and the
things you have prepared, whose will they be?' So is
the one who lays up treasure for himself and is not rich
toward God."

In this parable, the rich fool kept the excess of his material
wealth for himself, choosing to hoard it rather than give it away
during his lifetime. As a result, he was poor toward God; he did not
leverage his resources for eternal gain. His covetousness and stinginess
are two attributes that should not characterize any true believer, yet
even Christians, if we are not careful, can exhibit similar tendencies.

Hoarding our resources during this life and only giving them
away through our wills when we die stems partly from an illusion of
control. We want to provide for ourselves while we are alive, finding
temporary security and satisfaction in our wealth. This approach
neglects the fact that giving is, at its core, an act of faith, and thus
requires us to take the risk of entrusting ourselves *and* our gifts to
God. Releasing earthly treasure now (rather than later) demonstrates
our trust that God will provide for our needs and our recognition
that all wealth belongs to Him in the first place.

A popular rationale behind "cold-hand" giving is that waiting
to give will allow our money to have time to grow in major trust,
thus increasing the one-time amount we are able to give later. On
the surface, this seems sensible; however, if we dig a little deeper, we
uncover problems with this mindset.

First, "warm-hand" gifts can be immediately directed to a
vetted charitable entity (chapter 5 provides guidelines for vetting
these entities). There is no guarantee that an organization will last
until we die, so donating sooner rather than later allows us to provide
for immediate needs rather than potential needs. Also, just as with
other organizations, the mission of a foundation or trust can drift.
If we support their current aim, it is better to invest before they drift.

Second, the logic of waiting to give relies on earthly calculations
of risk and return rather than heavenly ones. Holding on to our money

instead of giving often stems from our desire to retain security for ourselves. The more money we have in our savings account, the more we feel we need to keep in order to have security (Ecclesiastes 5:10). The problem with this attitude is that with it we have succumbed to the gravitational pull of wealth. Money promises a security that it cannot give because there is no guarantee that it will last. There is also no guarantee that investing our money on earth will result only in increase and not in loss. What if, instead of focusing on what we could accomplish with five, ten, fifteen times more than we currently have, we think in the terms of kingdom metrics and ask, "What greater impact would this money have if we invest it in God's people now?" Who is to say that money given now won't experience greater growth by kingdom definitions?[8]

The Bible teaches the principle that giving generously now results in greater gain than saving it for later:

> One gives freely, yet grows all the richer; another withholds what he should give, and only suffers want.

> (Proverbs 11:24)

> Whoever sows sparingly will also reap sparingly, and whoever sows bountifully will also reap bountifully.

> (2 Corinthians 9:6)

The kingdom metrics in these two verses are the opposite of what the world tells us. But because God loves generosity, He blesses it with spiritual growth and a deepening intimacy with Him.

In addition, Jesus makes it clear in the parable of the talents in Matthew 25:14–30 that we grow in direct proportion to the risk we take in the service of God. In this parable, a man going on a journey entrusts his money to three of his servants and expects them to invest

---

8   For more on this, read the section in chapter 7 on reverse compounding.

this wealth wisely for him. Two of the servants do so, demonstrating faithfulness with what they have been given and doubling the amounts received, and the master gives them rewards proportionate to what they have done. The third servant, however, does nothing with the resources entrusted to him, and his master rebukes him for not investing the wealth wisely for some sort of gain. If we are to avoid making the same mistake as the foolish servant, we must use our resources wisely during our time on earth. After all, there is no guarantee our legatees will use the money we leave them for God's kingdom (Ecclesiastes 2:18–19).

Give as the Spirit Leads

Perhaps the most important principle of when to give is to listen to the promptings of the Holy Spirit. Paul commended the Macedonian churches for listening to the Spirit in their giving, saying that "they gave themselves first to the Lord and then by the will of God to us" (2 Corinthians 8:5). It is important to note the order of giving here: the Macedonians first dedicated themselves to God and listened to God's promptings on when to give, then gave generously to Paul for the saints in Jerusalem.

Another biblical example of giving as the Spirit leads occurs in Exodus 36:1–7. God commanded the people to give of their skills and resources as they were able for the construction of the tabernacle (vv. 2–3). The people listened to the promptings of the Spirit and ended up giving so generously that the workmen came to Moses and asked him to tell the people to stop giving (vv. 5–7)!

Listening to the promptings of the Spirit often leads us down paths that feel risky because they are countercultural and counterintuitive. The Israelites experienced this frequently in the Old Testament. God challenged them to give to Him *first*, and to wait and see what His provision would be (see Leviticus 25:1–7, 18–22; Malachi 3:10). Whenever the Israelites obeyed this command, God was faithful to His promises to them.

We see an example of God's faithfulness to His promises in 2 Kings 4:42–44, which says:

> A man came from Baal-shalishah, bringing the man
> of God bread of the firstfruits, twenty loaves of barley
> and fresh ears of grain in his sack. And Elisha said,
> "Give to the men, that they may eat." But his servant
> said, "How can I set this before a hundred men?" So he
> repeated, "Give them to the men, that they may eat, for
> thus says the Lord, 'They shall eat and have some left.'"
> So he set it before them. And they ate and had some
> left, according to the word of the Lord.

It's easy to rush through this short passage without recognizing how difficult and countercultural it was for the man from Baal-shalishah to bring his gift. Not only was there a severe famine in the land at the time, but the city this man came from was located in the northern kingdom of Israel, which at the time had almost completely succumbed to idolatry. This is evident even from the name of the city—Baal-shalishah, which means "three Baals" in Hebrew. Adding to the difficulty, the man did not have access to bring his offering to the temple since the northern kingdom had been cut off from Jerusalem, which was located in the southern kingdom.

With all these obstacles in the way, what did the man do? He obeyed God's commands to bring the firstfruits to Him as an act of worship in the only way he knew how—by bringing it to the prophet of the Lord, despite the fact that he had to travel across most of Israel to find him. He did not know what the result would be; he only knew that this was what God had called him to do. And the result was that God rewarded his faithfulness and multiplied his sacrifice. Elisha took the man's offering and told his servant to set it before the people who were with them. The servant was taken aback—there was not nearly enough to provide for everyone. But Elisha knew that God would reward faithfulness in listening to the promptings of the Spirit. And when the servant obeyed, there was more than enough left over.

As we have mentioned previously, we are not in the old covenant anymore and are not under the specific commandments to tithe our "firstfruits." However, God still rewards risk-taking as we obey the promptings of His Spirit instead of listening to our fears or the influence of our culture. There are numerous examples of Christians who have stepped out in faith and given sacrificially, only to then receive that same amount or more back! God may or may not choose to do this, but He does promise to provide us with everything we need, particularly so that we can continue to give generously to others. Paul makes this clear in 2 Corinthians 9:8–11:

> And God is able to make all grace abound to you, so that having all sufficiency in all things at all times, you may abound in every good work. As it is written,
>
> > "He has distributed freely, he has given to the poor; his righteousness endures forever."
>
> He who supplies seed to the sower and bread for food will supply and multiply your seed for sowing and increase the harvest of your righteousness. You will be enriched in every way to be generous in every way, which through us will produce thanksgiving to God.

God will enable us to obey the promptings of the Spirit, giving us everything we need to do so. And the result of this is that it will "produce thanksgiving to God"—not only your thanksgiving, but the thanksgiving of those to whom you have given. Giving generously may seem risky to us, but if it is truly what the Spirit is calling us to do, then it will bring God glory. After all, the greater the risk in the eyes of the world, the clearer it is that God is the One who provides all things (2 Corinthians 9:12–15).

It isn't always easy to listen to the Spirit, especially when He prompts us to give in a way that is uncomfortable to us—giving a large tip to our waiter, for example, or giving money to a complete stranger. At other times, God may call us to donate a large amount to a charity we've been researching or a church we've been attending when we would rather give a small amount or nothing at all. He may also call us to give an amount that seems impossible to us, but the truth is that we can't out-give God. He will provide the resources as we trust in His direction and will reward our faithfulness in participating in His kingdom purposes.

How do we know when the Spirit is prompting us to give? Although there is no set formula, the more we obey God, the easier it will be to hear Him clearly. Unfortunately, the inverse is also true: hardening our heart to God's promptings will make us less able to hear Him and know what He desires. As a result, we must train ourselves to pay attention to the Spirit, spending time in prayer and in the Word of God in order to become more sensitive to God's promptings.

The more we pray for opportunities to give, the more God will provide them. Just as He delights to give consistent, generous blessings to His children, so He delights when we act in accordance with His Spirit to do the same.

CHAPTER 3

How Are We to Give?

The Pharisees—the religious leaders during Jesus' day—gave generously and extravagantly. They kept the letter of the law in their giving, making sure to tithe even the smallest of garden herbs. However, instead of commending them, Jesus condemned them (see Matthew 23:1–39; Luke 11:37–54). Why? Because the amount of money is not ultimately what matters. Instead, it is *how* we give that matters.

The question of how we are to give could be answered in numerous ways, but this chapter zooms in on four key biblical principles: we are to give cheerfully, gratefully, anonymously, and harmoniously.

Give Cheerfully

Perhaps the most quoted verse about giving is 2 Corinthians 9:7: "Each one must give as he has decided in his heart, not reluctantly or under compulsion, for God loves a cheerful giver." The Pharisees gave out of compulsion, tithing in accordance with the law but not out of a cheerful spirit. They gave because they had to in order to appear pious, and in so doing they missed the joy that can come from generosity.

Just one chapter earlier in 2 Corinthians, Paul describes the cheerful, joyful spirit of the Macedonian churches:

> For in a severe test of affliction, their abundance of joy and their extreme poverty have overflowed in a wealth of generosity on their part. For they gave according to their means, as I can testify, and beyond their means, of their own accord, begging us earnestly for the favor of taking part in the relief of the saints.

> (2 Corinthians 8:2–4)

Joy characterized the generosity of the Macedonian churches. They did not see giving as a necessary evil or an unfortunate part of the Christian life. Instead, they *begged* to give despite their poverty. How was this possible?

Cheerful, sacrificial generosity is unthinkable apart from the work of the Holy Spirit. In verse 1 of the same chapter, we read about the grace of God that had been given to the Macedonians. He was the One who enabled them to feel such joy. In fact, both their joy and their generosity were His gifts to them.

If we are honest, our natural inclination is not to give out of our poverty but to amass wealth for ourselves as a means of security or for our satisfaction or to impress others. When we do give, it is often like prying open a tightly clenched fist. Even if we give large amounts of money, we tend to keep even larger sums back for ourselves. However, the more we give ourselves to God and become conformed to the image of Christ, the more cheerful and joyful we will become as we glorify God through the sacrifice of our wealth for those in need.

Give Gratefully

Although you've likely heard that God loves a cheerful giver, you may not have considered that cheerful giving stems from a posture of gratitude. We give cheerfully when we are full of gratitude for what God has done for us. Going back to the example of the Macedonian churches, Paul reveals that they gave abundantly and cheerfully because they were intimately acquainted with the work of Christ on their behalf (2 Corinthians 8:9).

In order to give as God intends, we must first appreciate the depth and vastness of the gifts we ourselves have been given. In Christ we have "every spiritual blessing in the heavenly places" (Ephesians 1:3), and God has shown us the "immeasurable riches of his grace in kindness toward us" (Ephesians 2:7). We feast on the abundance of God's house, drinking from the river of delights that He provides for us (Psalm 36:8). Not only that, but we have abundant life in Christ (John 10:10). Life will not be easy—in fact, Jesus tells us that we will experience adversity (John 16:33)—but we have "an inheritance that is imperishable, undefiled, and unfading, kept in heaven for [us]" (1 Peter 1:4). Our security on earth comes not from our financial resources but from the eternal treasure we have in Christ. In all circumstances, then, we can give thanks to God and demonstrate our gratitude through cheerful, generous giving (Philippians 4:11–13).

Not only do we give gratefully because of our inheritance in Christ, but we give gratefully because the Holy Spirit enables us to do so. There is nothing we have that we did not receive from God—and that includes gratitude (1 Corinthians 4:7). The Spirit is the One who works in our hearts to enable to us to give gratefully in the first place. Because we are in Christ, we are no longer ruled by our sinful desires (Romans 6:6). The Spirit gives us a new heart (Jeremiah 31:31–34; Hebrews 8:8–12) so that our lives are now marked by a profound sense of gratitude for the One who rescued us from our sin and gave us everything in Him. As a result, we give gratefully not only of our resources, but of our whole being (Romans 12:1).

Once we recognize that we have everything in Christ and that even generous, grateful giving comes from Him, we experience more gratitude that flows from grasping what an absolute privilege it is to participate in God's kingdom endeavor. Just think: the God of the universe invites *us* to be part of something that will echo through the caverns of eternity! Although financial generosity (or any other good work) does not secure our salvation (Ephesians 2:8–9), we as believers are nevertheless enriched by our acts of faith: "Whoever sows sparingly will also reap sparingly, and whoever sows bountifully will also reap bountifully" (2 Corinthians 9:6). In essence, giving is a multiplier; it takes a seed and grows it to the tangible benefit of the recipient and the spiritual benefit of the giver.

While cheerfulness and gratitude are key components of giving with an open hand and a God-oriented heart, they are undoubtedly elusive virtues; unless reinforced and enhanced intentionally, they diminish over time. If we regard gratitude as nothing more than a feeling instead of an intentional choice, it will quickly flee. However, by bringing to remembrance God's provision in the past, benefits in the present, and promises for the future, we will be able to develop a posture of gratitude in all that we do, including in our financial generosity.

Give Anonymously

When our lives are marked by gratitude and we recognize that we have nothing that we did not receive from God, we are also able to give in a third way commanded in the Bible: anonymously. Jesus delineates this principle in Matthew 6:2–4:

> Thus, when you give to the needy, sound no trumpet before you, as the hypocrites do in the synagogues and in the streets, that they may be praised by others. Truly, I say to you, they have received their reward. But when you give to the needy, do not let your left hand know what your right hand is doing, so that your giving may be in secret. And your Father who sees in secret will reward you.

God commands us in no uncertain terms to exercise our faith without pomp and vanity. We are to do things before Him and not for public recognition. God understands well our desire for public recognition when doing good or faithful deeds, but such a desire stems from an egocentric focus rather than a focus on the Giver of all good gifts (James 1:17). Focusing on the betterment of others rather than the bolstering of ourselves requires a posture of humility, which means surrendering our wills to God and acknowledging that He is the One who gives all things. The wealth we give away is His in the first place; we are merely stewards entrusted with His resources.

Anonymous giving offers numerous benefits in our stewardship before God.[9] To name just a few, it rightfully assigns all honor and glory to God, who is the ultimate source of provision; it reduces our temptation to give from the selfish motives of seeking reciprocity and personal gain; and it protects the dignity of the giver-recipient relationship by preventing the latter from mistaking the former as the agent of provision rather than as a conduit of God's grace. In sum, anonymous giving teaches people to look to God instead of currying favor with a human being.

Another benefit of giving anonymously is that it guards us against a sense of entitlement when we give away our money. When we donate a large sum to our local church, for example, it can be easy to think we should have more say than others in the church's decisions. This is explicitly condemned in James 2:1–9, which tells us that we must have no partiality based on wealth. Anonymous giving helps protect us from this partiality, reminding us that God is the One who owns our resources, and we are simply stewarding His gifts to us.

Give Harmoniously

Although many Christians agree on the three principles of giving cheerfully, gratefully, and anonymously, there is a fourth principle not often discussed: giving harmoniously. Harmonious giving occurs in the narrower context of marriage as well as in the wider context of the local church.

---

9 See chapter 10 for how a donor-advised fund (DAF) can assist in giving anonymously.

Giving Harmoniously in Marriage

One of the biggest causes of divorce is financial disagreement—and this is true for Christians and non-Christians alike. However, God has called us to unity in marriage as a picture of His perfect union with us. The way we treat our finances is no exception. In light of this, how should we navigate the difficulties of giving harmoniously when our spouse disagrees with us?

First of all, let me acknowledge that the answer to this question is especially difficult to answer when one spouse is a Christian and the other is not. The Bible does not give clear commands on this, but it *does* outline the principle that we are to be the aroma of Christ to unbelievers—and that includes an unbelieving spouse (2 Corinthians 2:15). It is wise to seek financial counsel together from an external source when one spouse wants to give to further God's kingdom and the other does not. It may be that you need to explain to your spouse why such giving is important to you, give a smaller amount than you normally would, or perhaps give toward a mission/ministry about which you both can agree. In these situations, continue to pray for the salvation of your spouse as well as for God to give you unity in your finances.

Even when both spouses are Christians, financial disagreements are common. Often, one spouse will want to be more cautious and the other will want to take more risks. When making money decisions in marriage, the best approach is to honor one another by listening carefully and showing genuine respect for one another, even in the midst of disagreement. In such a way, we fulfill what Paul says in Philippians 2:1–4:

> So if there is any encouragement in Christ, any comfort from love, any participation in the Spirit, any affection and sympathy, complete my joy by being of the same mind, having the same love, being in full accord and of one mind. Do nothing from selfish ambition or conceit, but in humility count others more significant than yourselves. Let each of you look not only to his own interests, but also to the interests of others.

This commitment to partnership builds greater mutuality, trust, and wisdom. Of course, as much as we would like to come to an agreement whenever we argue, in this fallen world we will not always be of the same mind. Although we'd each like to get our own way every time, this outcome would be to the dyad's detriment. We need to walk in humility, putting the desires of our spouse above our own.

The simplest way to maintain unity through harmonious giving is by having a plan in place before a disagreement arises. If you are dating with a goal of marriage or if you are engaged, talk over finances with your significant other now and pray for generosity together. If you are already married, pray with your spouse, making a point to come before God regularly and ask Him to give you unity in your desires to give. Create a budget *together* and be willing to compromise. If one spouse is comfortable with giving less, it may be wise to go with that lesser amount for a time. Keeping a good record of your finances can help you see the margin in your budget and notice God's faithfulness to provide for your needs.

As you pray with your spouse, consider walking through the following questions with one another:

- What did your giving look like before marriage?
- Why are you hesitant to give?
- What would make you agree on an amount to give?
- Do you want to see a financial advisor or counselor to help work through your finances?

Keep in mind that God is always growing both you and your spouse, but He may do so in different ways and at different rates. Giving together will not only increase your fellowship with your spouse, but it will reflect the glory of God and provide a good witness to those around you.

Giving Harmoniously as a Church

In a wider context, we are also to give harmoniously as a church. Chances are, if you ask most Christians about church giving, they will probably think about members of a local church giving enough to cover the pastor's salary, the upkeep of the church building, and various costs for church ministry programs. These are important (and we'll go into this more in chapter 5), but they revolve around giving *to* the church. If this is all we think about, we overlook the biblical principle that we are also called to give *as* a church.

We see a clear example of this principle in Scripture through Paul's collection for the saints at Jerusalem. Apparently, the Christians in Jerusalem were having trouble providing for their basic needs, probably due to persecution. Paul began instructing the churches where he had ministered to store up money so he could deliver it when he returned to Jerusalem (1 Corinthians 16:1; 2 Corinthians 9:1–5). When he did so, he addressed his commands to the churches as a whole, not just to individual believers.

Why did Paul think it was so important for entire churches to give harmoniously, rather than giving only as individuals? His instructions about the collection reveal two main reasons.

First, giving harmoniously as a church underscores the essential unity of the body of believers (Romans 15:27; Philippians 4:14). Paul tells the Corinthians that one of the results of their financial gift is that the recipients will, "by prayer on your behalf, yearn for you because of the surpassing grace of God in you" (2 Corinthians 9:14 NASB).

Think about Paul's context for a moment. Most of the Corinthian believers were Gentiles, whereas most of the believers in Jerusalem were Jewish. The relationship between Jewish and Gentile believers in the first century was not always peaceful. As a result, when writing 2 Corinthians, Paul was concerned about more than the physical needs of the Jewish believers in Jerusalem. He also saw the collection as an opportunity for the Gentile churches to demonstrate their "eager[ness] to maintain the unity of the Spirit in the bond of peace" (Ephesians 4:3). It was a much greater witness for the Gentile churches to give harmoniously than it would have been if a few wealthy Corinthians had individually sent the funds needed for the believers in Jerusalem.

The second reason Paul commands churches to give harmoniously is because it brings glory to God. He writes in 2 Corinthians 9:12–13:

> For the ministry of this service is not only supplying the needs of the saints but is also overflowing in many thanksgivings to God. By their approval of this service, they will glorify God because of your submission that comes from your confession of the gospel of Christ, and the generosity of your contribution for them and for all others.

Harmonious giving results in the recipient thanking God, not for the gift itself, but for the giving church's faithfulness to the gospel. Paul himself glorified God because of the Philippian church's repeated contribution to his own ministry. He did so because he was overjoyed at the fruitfulness of the Philippians' faith (Philippians 4:17).

Although churches look different today than in Paul's day (after all, there is no "Church of Atlanta, Georgia" or "Church of Greenville, South Carolina" like there was a church at Philippi or at Ephesus), this principle of giving as a church remains the same. When we are part of a local congregation, we ought to know how the church is using its financial resources. Even though church structures differ—in some cases, the leadership will decide where to give, whereas in other churches the congregation is more actively involved—its members should be in agreement as to the way the church is spending its money. A good principle here is to make sure the money is being used to further the gospel in some way, whether for the needs of the saints or for the spreading of the gospel (we'll go deeper into this in chapter 5).

A practical advantage to giving as a church as we further the gospel is the ability to pool our resources as a congregation and support, for example, one or more missionaries full time in a stable manner. As we discussed in chapter 2, providing consistently for missionaries allows them to spread the gospel more securely, knowing their material needs have been met. This is exactly what the Philippian church did for Paul. They "entered into partnership with [him] in giving and receiving" (Philippians 4:15). As a result, Paul was able to report, "I have received full payment, and more. I am well supplied" (v. 18).

Now, we can (and should!) give generously for the sake of the gospel through our individual giving, but if we only ever give as individuals and never as a church, we are missing out on the spiritual blessings of harmonious giving. God delights in the unity of His people, and our harmonious giving glorifies His name as we proclaim the gospel.

CHAPTER 4

How Much Are We to Give?

If we're honest, instead of thinking "How *much* can I give?", many of us are probably guilty of the mindset "How *little* can I get away with giving?" When we assess our financial situations, we are more likely to consider how much we want to keep before pondering how much we can give away. This tendency is a result of the Fall. Instead of remembering that we are stewards of all God has graciously given us, we pursue control through our financial kingdoms. Rather than seek the benefit of others, we look to our own luxury and personal enhancement first before giving away any of our resources.

The good news is that God is more than able to break the power money holds over us, relegating it to its proper place as a means of glorifying Him instead of a dead idol to which we are enslaved. In filling us with His Spirit, He calls us to a radical way of living, one that demonstrates dependence on the eternal God through giving that is both proportionate and sacrificial.

Give Proportionately

If you hear the words "proportionate giving," chances are you automatically think of a 10 percent tithe. While this amount of giving can be a good standard to put into practice, generosity in the Bible encompasses much more than a set amount of money to give.

The idea of the 10 percent tithe stems from the Levitical tithe in the Old Testament. This tithe mandated that the Israelites give 10 percent of their income to the Levites because the Levites had no inheritance in the Promised Land; they were set apart for God's service and for the care of the public worship system (Numbers 18:21, 24). The Levites maintained the tabernacle and later the temple, performing various tasks in order to assist the people with their sacrifices. In essence, this tithe provided for the Old Testament equivalent of church services, leading many Christians to see this tithe continuing through the modern local church. Those who hold to this tithe today give 10 percent of their income to the church they attend in order to maintain the building, provide for the staff, hold regular services, and support the giving endeavors of the church itself.

While giving 10 percent to the church is a good thing, the principle of generous giving actually goes deeper than this. As we discussed in chapter 2, there are three active tithes and one passive tithe mentioned in the Old Testament. In addition to the Levitical tithe, the Israelites also had the tithe of the feasts (Deuteronomy 14:22–27) and the poor tithe (Deuteronomy 14:28–29). The tithe of the feasts was a yearly celebration in which the people took 10 percent of their firstfruits and the firstborn of their animals in order to feast before the Lord and praise Him for His goodness and provision. The poor tithe occurred once every three years, mandating that the Israelites care for those in need in their society. The Old Testament also mentions a passive tithe in which the Israelites left the gleanings of their fields for the poor of the land, passing over what likely amounted to around 10 percent of their harvest.

In terms of proportionate giving, based on these four tithes, the Israelites gave around 33 percent of their income on a yearly basis, along with any additional sacrifices they desired to make. This far exceeds the 10 percent tithe that many of us regard as satisfactory! Although we are no longer under the Mosaic Law of the old covenant system, the principle of proportionate giving—giving according to ability—still continues in the new covenant. Paul reiterates this principle in 2 Corinthians 8:12–14:

> For if the readiness is there, it is acceptable according to what a person has, not according to what he does not have. For I do not mean that others should be eased and you burdened, but that as a matter of fairness your abundance at the present time should supply their need, so that their abundance may supply your need, that there may be fairness.

In this passage, Paul exhorts the Corinthians to give based on what they have—in other words, to give proportionately, or according to ability. While giving above and beyond our means is also commended in certain situations (2 Corinthians 8:3), Paul does not want to put undue pressure on anyone to give more than they are able. For some, that amount may look like a 10 percent tithe of their income. For others, that amount can and should be much higher. Proportionality is the notion is that the more we have, the more we can give away.

We would like this principle to be simple, to have the Bible give us a specific amount that is "enough" to give away, but the fact of the matter is that Scripture doesn't give us exact instructions. Instead, it gives us principles and leaves how much we give to our discernment as we listen to God's call and follow His will. When we seek His guidance, the Spirit will convict us, leading us to make a thought-out resolution between ourselves and God that governs our behavior regarding our finances. The problem is, our own wills often get in the way of doing so, making it difficult to obey when He calls us. We must make a practice of trust, obedience, and submission to the Father in order to overcome the temptation to give superficially.

We must make a practice of trust, obedience, and submission to the Father in order to overcome the temptation to give superficially.

Over the years, I tried an experiment regarding proportionate giving. Every year, I bumped up the percentage of my giving. I found myself slowly acclimating to greater risk as time went on, and it became easier to increase the sum I was giving. When we see how God continues to show up and take care of us, we become more inclined to take these material risks and invest in His eternal kingdom.

There is a good deal of room for the power of the Holy Spirit to show us how much God wants us to give. God is the One providing our financial resources; He can increase or decrease the amount of wealth we have. When He does so, He still expects us to trust Him with our resources, listening to the guidance of the Spirit. Instead of choosing to hoard money from a larger paycheck, we can ask the Spirit to help us view it as an opportunity to give more abundantly and provide for someone else's need. If our paycheck decreases, we should still submit to the Spirit's guidance as we give, trusting that God will provide for us as we follow His call. Or, if our wealth comes mainly from our assets or net worth, we can give out of those as the Spirit leads us. The key to proportionate giving is relying on the Spirit and trusting God with our finances, prayerfully asking Him what He wants us to do with the money He has given us.

Give Sacrificially

Proportionate giving is biblical, but it's only one aspect of what the Bible has to say on how much we are to give. The Bible also commands us to give *sacrificially* in order to glorify God and further the spread of His kingdom. When we are miserly with our wealth, thinking in terms of how much we can keep rather than how much we can give, our witness to others as well as our own spiritual growth is hindered. Because God generously gave up His own Son for our sake, He calls us to give up everything to follow Jesus (Luke 9:23). No matter our income bracket, we have the opportunity to give sacrificially out of gratitude for what God has done for us, glorifying Him with our finances.

Jesus' Radical Call to Sacrificial Giving

One of the major heresies in our time is the "prosperity gospel," a false teaching inherently opposed to sacrificial giving. Whereas Scripture tells us to give generously and sacrificially, this heresy views Jesus as a means to a material end. Follow Jesus, it claims, and He will bless you with health and wealth. Believe and you will receive, name it and claim it, and whatever material goods you desire will be yours. Often citing old covenant promises about material blessing out of their redemptive historical context (for example, 1 Chronicles 4:10 or Malachi 3:10),[10]

---

10 Proponents of the prosperity gospel often cite passages in the Old Testament to support their views that God will bless His followers materially in whatever ways they ask. If the Israelites gave the tithes commanded, God promised in the old covenant to bless them materially. Such a blessing was supposed to result in the Israelites giving all the more cheerfully and sacrificially as part of their worship, beautifying the temple and supplying more sacrifices as they saw that God provided for their needs. He would make a way for them to continue to give more and more generously as they obeyed His call (see Proverbs 11:24–25). In such a way, God would distinguish between His covenant people and the foreign nations, showing that His hand alone provides material blessings.

While God can—and does—reward our material generosity, we are now living in a different part of redemptive history, and that comes with different manifestations of His promises. No longer does God promise to bless us materially for following Him (even though He sometimes chooses to do so). Instead, the call has become even more radical, as the story of the rich young man makes clear in Mark 10:17–31.

For more on this, listen to David Platt's sermon "Jesus and Money," which can be accessed at radical.net/message/jesus-and-money.

this dangerous vein of thinking places more value on earthly goods than on the spiritual joy of following Jesus no matter the cost.

Now, it is true that God often chooses to bless His people in material ways and that He desires us to enjoy those material blessings, but we also need to remember God's call to give sacrificially and the temptations that come with being rich. We are not *entitled* to the wealth God gives us; we are *entrusted* with it. And if He calls us to give it all up to follow Him, then we need to be prepared to do so, no matter the cost to us. The problem is not the wealth itself; it is our valuation of wealth above God.

Jesus' encounter with the rich young man in Mark 10:17–31 makes this clear. In this account, a religious young man approached Jesus and asked what he must do to inherit eternal life. Jesus told him to keep the commandments, and the rich young man asserted that he had done so. Mark relates what happened next:

> And Jesus, looking at him, loved him, and said to him, "You lack one thing: go, sell all that you have and give to the poor, and you will have treasure in heaven; and come, follow me." Disheartened by the saying, he went away sorrowful, for he had great possessions.
>
> (Mark 10:21–22)

Jesus gave this man one costly command—to sell all his possessions—*but the man went away sorrowful.* Even though he followed God on other accounts, his numerous possessions had become a stumbling block to him. He valued them more than he valued Jesus. This is the same danger we need to be aware of in our own lives, particularly if we have an abundance of possessions.

Now, I can hear what you are thinking—*God doesn't call everyone to sell all of their possessions and give everything to the poor.* That is true. God has a unique calling for each of our lives, and He does choose to bless some of us abundantly with material possessions that He graciously allows us to keep and enjoy. But don't miss this: He just might call *you* to give up everything. If God asks you to do this, would you be willing? If not, then you are still viewing your possessions as your own and not as God's to do with what He will.

When we think about how much Jesus asked the rich man to give up, it's easy to forget why the text says he did this—*because He loved him*. He wanted the man to give up all his *worldly* goods for his *ultimate* good. He wanted the man to give up *earthly* treasure for *heavenly* treasure. The man may have kept his possessions, but he lost something of far greater value. In this same passage, Jesus tells His disciples that anyone who gives up something for the sake of the gospel will "receive a hundredfold now in this time" (Mark 10:30). For whatever we give away for the sake of following and obeying Jesus, we receive reward in the present age. This reward is a spiritual benefit—greater intimacy with Christ and greater spiritual growth.

Trusting God Through Sacrificial Giving

Our greatest good does not come from storing up treasure on earth, but it can be easy to accidentally put our hope in wealth. Money is not neutral; it has a downward pull. The more wealth we have, the harder it is to trust God and give sacrificially, just like it was for the man in Mark 10. In fact, we may even *think* we are giving sacrificially when we can afford to give much more.

This stems partly from a lack of contentment in Christ. No matter where we fall on the spectrum of annual income, we tend to think in terms of comparison: "I make $30,000 a year, but *he* makes $50,000, so I'm not rich," or "I make $1,000,000 a year, but *she* makes $6,000,000, so I'm not rich." The reality is that the majority of people reading this book have more than enough to provide for their basic needs and then some.

In order to recognize the downward pull of wealth and the evil that comes from our discontentment, we need to hear what Paul writes in 1 Timothy 6:8–10:

> But if we have food and clothing, with these we will be content. But those who desire to be rich fall into temptation, into a snare, into many senseless and harmful

desires that plunge people into ruin and destruction.
For the love of money is a root of all kinds of evils. It
is through this craving that some have wandered away
from the faith and pierced themselves with many pangs.

Even though we should be content with having our basic needs
provided for, the desire to have *more* affects everyone. Those with a
lower income may be tempted to hold on to their wealth until they
feel they have reached a place where they can afford to give without
feeling the pinch. Those with a higher income may struggle with
sacrificial giving because they define themselves by the quantifiable
measurements of wealth and possessions. But sacrificial giving is costly
giving. It requires that we give up our desire to hold on to wealth for
earthly gain and give what God calls us to give. It is a reorientation
that reminds us that no matter the amount of wealth we have, it all
belongs to God.

In giving sacrificially, we need to remember that it is not ultimately the *amount* of money we give that matters, but the *heart* behind
the giving. Consider the story of sacrificial giving in Luke 21:1–4:

> Jesus looked up and saw the rich putting their gifts
> into the offering box, and he saw a poor widow put in
> two small copper coins. And he said, "Truly, I tell you,
> this poor widow has put in more than all of them. For
> they all contributed out of their abundance, but she
> out of her poverty put in all she had to live on."

This story demonstrates how proportionate and sacrificial giving
are interrelated in Scripture: The rich proportionately gave much less
than the widow, even though the sums they deposited into the offering
box were much larger. They gave out of their abundance; the widow gave
out of her poverty. Proportionately speaking, the rich were not affected
at all by their offerings and could continue with their luxurious lifestyle
without pinching pennies, which demonstrates that they gave superficially
rather than sacrificially. Sacrificial giving, after all, is not tied to a specific

amount or percentage. As a result, although the widow's offering of two small copper coins is a gift that would seem meager to many, Jesus tells us that her offering was worth more. It wasn't the amount given that mattered to Jesus; it was the giver's heart of generosity and sacrificial love for Him. The rich gave as part of their religious façade; the widow gave out of a heart of worship. They gave only a small part of their material blessings; she gave everything she had to live on.

Now, once again, while we are called to give sacrificially, this does not mean we have to give everything we own. As we mentioned earlier in the chapter, God calls us to give proportionately based on what we have (2 Corinthians 8:12–14). The key to giving sacrificially and proportionately is obeying the promptings of the Holy Spirit and giving as much as He leads us to give—*even if it is everything we own.* We see this through the difficult example of Ananias and Sapphira in Acts 5. The members of the early church were living with everything in common, providing for one another financially (Acts 2:42–47). During this time, a man named Joseph (also called Barnabas) sold a field that he owned and gave the entire proceeds to the apostles (Acts 4:36–37). Ananias and Sapphira observed this, and they decided to do the same thing—with a catch. Instead of giving everything, they chose to hold something back for themselves and merely pretend to give everything. When they brought it before Peter, he confronted them, saying:

> Ananias, why has Satan filled your heart to lie to the Holy Spirit and to keep back for yourself part of the proceeds of the land? While it remained unsold, did it not remain your own? And after it was sold, was it not at your disposal? Why is it that you have contrived this deed in your heart? You have not lied to man but to God.

> (Acts 5:3–4)

Notice that Peter did not condemn Ananias and Sapphira for keeping some of the money for themselves. In fact, he told them they were welcome to do so! But he *did* condemn them for lying to

God. This couple's heart was in the wrong place. They wanted to be seen and commended, and so they lied. Instead of having a sacrificial mindset, they were seeking to please people and were secretly looking out for themselves. The result was that they ended up lying to God—a fatal mistake. Likewise, we need to be on guard against a desire for earthly gain at the cost of our spiritual welfare. As we do so, we need to remember that when we give sacrificially, we are only losing temporary riches, but we are gaining eternal wealth in Christ.

Sacrificial Giving as Stewardship

As we seek to give sacrificially, a good diagnostic tool is to consider what we are giving up to invest in God's kingdom. Simply writing a check is not enough, especially if we use it as a means to ease our conscience when God is calling us to give more. If our desire for luxury and personal enhancement interferes with our desire to give sacrificially, we need to prayerfully ask God what He wants us to give and obey Him. Sacrificial giving will be costly in terms of earthly treasure, but it reminds us that God is the One who owns our financial resources. We are merely stewards and ambassadors using the funds He has provided us for His kingdom work. Everything—our finances, our time, even the very breath we take moment by moment—belongs to God and is a gift to us. This truth should be freeing. We do not need to hold on to excess wealth in order to provide for ourselves because the God who created the universe cares enough for us to provide for us, and we can trust Him!

This truth is harder for us to accept the more wealth we have (Ecclesiastes 5:10). We tend to find security or satisfaction in our wealth without even realizing that we do so. With a large income, we may give away $100,000 but keep back for ourselves $1,000,000 without ever seeking God's direction. We may donate $1,000,000 but allow ourselves the privilege of owning a second house, a garage of extra cars, or any number of luxuries without first consulting God and asking if this is how He would have us use what He has entrusted to us. As disciples of Jesus (and this isn't easy!) we must be willing to humbly and honestly ask God to direct our financial decisions with a heart that is ready to respond with obedience however He leads. In the end, sacrificial giving is not about developing rigid rules or pharisaical laws to legislate how we use money. Instead, it is about cultivating a heart that trusts God and is willing to gladly yield to His leading.

As we examine our financial situations, our first tendency is often to make excuses for why we keep material wealth. One excuse we often make is that we need extra wealth to provide for every possible contingency. While it is wise to plan for the future, we simply cannot prepare for all the "what ifs" of life. Trying to store up money to soothe our anxieties will interfere with our ability to give *now* to meet current needs. God gave us gifts to use and release, not to hoard. Worry about wealth reveals that we are serving money as our master (Matthew 6:24). This is why Jesus told us, "It is easier for a camel to go through the eye of a needle than for a rich person to enter the kingdom of God" (Mark 10:25). But there is good news! When Jesus' disciples responded to this statement in utter amazement, wondering who can be saved with such high standards, Jesus said, "With man it is impossible, but not with God. For all things are possible with God" (v. 27).

Sacrificial Giving as Worship

If we ask Him, God is gracious to give us a heart that desires to give sacrificially. When we come to understand that Jesus has done everything for us and given of Himself sacrificially—in fact, He gave up riches we cannot imagine—then it only makes sense that we will give sacrificially. God may choose to bless us materially, but that is nothing compared with the spiritual blessings He has given us. When it comes down to it, He offers us *everything* in Him—and that is why giving away material goods results only in gain.

If we are giving sacrificially out of a right spirit, then we are using our finances as a means of worshiping God. We see this worship illustrated in Matthew 26:6–13 (paralleled in Mark 14:3–9 and John 12:1–8). While Jesus was eating at the house of Simon the leper with His disciples, a woman came up to Him and broke a very expensive jar of pure nard over His head. Note that perfume bottles were different in

Jesus' day than the ones we have now. Whereas we can store perfume in a bottle that dispenses it slowly, back then the jar had to be broken open and the fragrance could only be used once. By breaking open the jar of perfume, this woman was extravagantly worshiping Jesus through an expensive financial resource. The disciples condemned her for it, saying that the money could have been given to the poor, but they missed the worship involved in her sacrifice. This sinful woman knew that Jesus was the One to whom all honor was due, and she glorified Him through this costly act.

Giving sacrificially stems from the security we have in Christ's extravagant goodness toward us. In Him, we have "every spiritual blessing in the heavenly places" (Ephesians 1:3) and "every good gift and every perfect gift [that] is from above" (James 1:17). For our sake, Jesus, "though he was in the form of God, did not count equality with God a thing to be grasped, but emptied himself, by taking the form of a servant, being born in the likeness of men. And being found in human form, he humbled himself by becoming obedient to the point of death, even death on a cross" (Philippians 2:6–8). Jesus, "though he was rich, yet for your sake he became poor, so that you by his poverty might become rich" (2 Corinthians 8:9).

As we look to the example of Christ and entrust ourselves to Him, He will work in our hearts to progressively mold us into His image. As He does so, we will give sacrificially. When we demonstrate the radical trust of obeying Him, running the apparent risk of losing everything from a worldly standpoint, we will actually gain everything. This security enables us to give more and more sacrificially out of a posture of humility and gratitude.

CHAPTER 5

Where Are We to Give?

It's no secret that for many, the decision of where to give is closely intertwined with the question of tax deductibility. But while it is wise to make financial decisions strategically and with due diligence, financial benefits should not be the only factor we consider (see chapter 7 for some of the factors to take into account). Instead, we need to decide where to give by listening to the prompting of the Holy Spirit and, in doing so, ensure that our giving is in accordance with the Great Commission.

Spirit-Led Giving

Wisdom in the financial sphere of our lives, as in all other spheres, increases proportionately with our responsiveness to the prompting of the Spirit. Without training, we will automatically fall into the way of the world, which defines us by default. But through diligent practice, we can learn to resist the natural human tendency to either run ahead or lag behind the Spirit, choosing instead a posture of obedient attunement.

When it comes to giving, God desires that we give where He leads with a cheerful heart. And the good news is, He is more than able to do this work in us: "And God is able to make all grace abound to you, so that having all sufficiency in all things at all times, you may abound in every good work" (2 Corinthians 9:8). If we ask Him, God will surely guide us and provide opportunities for financial generosity. He will direct our steps as we faithfully approach Him in prayer.

One example of how the Spirit might lead us is when a name pops into our minds seemingly out of the blue—perhaps in a dream or while we are engaged in an unrelated task. When this happens, it may well be that God is placing an individual, family, or organization on our hearts so that we can use the resources He has given us to offer them support in their time of need.

Many years ago, when my wife, Karen, and I lived in England, God put two widows on our minds in this very manner. We felt strongly called to support them and ended up sending them annual gifts over several decades. We wanted to respond faithfully to a call to give, in the hope that it would enrich these women's lives and point them to God. We gave to them in the name of Jesus and left the rest in God's hands.

As we practice heeding the promptings of the Spirit, we will naturally develop personalized approaches to giving. Because it helps me to have a visual array of options when deciding where to give, I keep in my desk a set of giving envelopes from various ministries and friends; I sometimes review and pray over these to help me discern where to give. This process of prayerful discernment is ongoing; every time I respond appropriately to the promptings of the Spirit, that act of faith amplifies the sound of the Spirit the next time, making it easier for me to hear and obey Him. The converse is also true; ignoring the Spirit makes me less sensitive to His instruction.

As we pray in the power of the Spirit, we also need to make sure we are carefully researching the charitable entities where we are considering giving. Some nonprofits—especially unaccredited ones—keep back large portions of the donations they receive for their own staff. Others may not have the ability to reach the intended recipients. Still others are scams set up to steal money. We should be cautious when giving, investigating the charitable entity we choose. At the same time, these exceptions to true charities should not cause us to stem the flow of our giving. We need to be wise as well as generous (cf. Matthew 10:16), listening to the Spirit and giving as we receive a call from Him.

As you discern where to give according to the call of the Spirit, consider praying through the following questions:[11]

- Where is the Lord leading me to give?
- Am I giving to my local church? If not, why not?
- Are there any local ministries or organizations I am connected with or passionate about?
- Are there any new ministries/organizations I should consider?
- Is God calling me to give to a different area of ministry?
- Are there certain areas of the world beyond my local community where I sense God wants me to focus? Do I have connections abroad, to either an organization or an individual?
- Is God calling me to give more to organizations, to individuals in need, or to specific projects?

I have learned over the years that not every need is a call from God. In situations when we might feel pulled in multiple directions or overwhelmed by the sheer amount of need, it is

---

11   Questions adapted from Ronald Blue Trust resources.

always wise to pray for God to give us specificity. Our giving will change depending on our season of life. We learn this from the example of the Philippians. Although they desired to aid Paul and were concerned for his well-being, it took time before they had an opportunity to provide for him (Philippians 4:10). As soon as they were able to do so, they gave financially toward his missionary journeys to support him. Likewise, if there seems to be something blocking our donations toward a particular cause, we can wait, pray over where to give, and continue to set aside financial resources in the meantime (1 Corinthians 16:1–3). This is not an indefinite suspension of giving—we still need to be generous while we wait— but it is a wise course of action as we pray over a specific cause. If we are still uncertain after doing so, we can also seek counsel from godly Christians around us, asking them to pray that we would have wisdom in our financial giving.

Giving Toward the Great Commission

One test to determine where the Spirit is leading us to give is to see if it lines up in some way with the Great Commission:

> And Jesus came and said to them, "All authority in heaven and on earth has been given to me. Go there-fore and make disciples of all nations, baptizing them in the name of the Father and of the Son and of the Holy Spirit, teaching them to observe all that I have commanded you. And behold, I am with you always, to the end of the age."
>
> (Matthew 28:18–20)

This directive is surprisingly dynamic. The commands in this passage to go, to baptize, and to teach modify the main command: *to make disciples*. Becoming a disciple—a follower of Jesus whose life becomes increasingly conformed to His image—is God's ultimate purpose for us in this soul-forming world. Once we have become disciples, we are to go and disciple others as well. Thus, disciple-making should drive our financial decisions.

When we think about discipleship entities, what usually comes to mind is the local church. As we discussed earlier, this is a good place to give—in fact, Paul essentially commands us to do so:

> Do you not know that those who are employed in the temple service get their food from the temple, and those who serve at the altar share in the sacrificial offerings? In the same way, the Lord commanded that those who proclaim the gospel should get their living by the gospel.
>
> (1 Corinthians 9:13–14)

> Let the one who is taught the word share all good things with the one who teaches.
>
> (Galatians 6:6)

> For the Scripture says, "You shall not muzzle an ox when it treads out the grain," and, "The laborer deserves his wages."
>
> (1 Timothy 5:18)

It is beneficial for us to provide financially for the needs of the local church because the church is the main place in which the Word of God is preached and Christians are discipled. At the same time, it is important to note that the local church should not serve as a mere storehouse for monetary gifts from which it draws to sustain its infrastructural growth, but as a redistribution point. In other words, the church should not be so focused on material items that it neglects spiritual matters.[12] It needs to be using the money it collects on behalf of those actively teaching or furthering the gospel—usually a pastor, staff member, or missionary.[13]

We see this financial role of the church in the life of Paul. Various churches supported him in his missionary efforts, enabling him to travel and preach the gospel. The Philippian church in particular was generous with its funds, choosing to give to him when it had the opportunity (Philippians 4:14–17). As we discussed in chapter 3, it is certainly good for individuals to give directly to missionaries and teachers. However, there are also advantages to the church as a whole giving to support missionaries. For one thing, a church's commitment to give consistently provides more financial stability to missionaries. For another, giving *to* the church and *as* a church promotes unity among believers (see Philippians 2:2).

In addition to giving to missionaries, the church can also support various ministries by giving to those in need. Note that it is not the role of the church to support every kind of ministry or supply every kind of need—unlike in the times of the apostles, many governments do have various charities or programs available to meet needs. However, the church should still be actively involved in ministering to those with various physical needs, particularly Christians. Paul advocated for this when he ordered the collection for the poor among the saints at Jerusalem (see Romans 15:26). In

---

12   One of the common pitfalls among churches is the search for a new or better building. While it can be beneficial for a local church to have its own building, God will provide in due season. Many churches lay out extravagant plans for expensive new buildings when it would be better to rent or purchase a simpler building and use their finances for the spreading of the gospel. Other churches claim that they will begin redistributing their finances after their own material needs have been abundantly provided for. But God calls us as churches to give now, not later, and to do ministry even in difficult situations. The early churches, after all, met in the homes of believers, and it is important to remember that the church is ultimately the Body of Christ rather than a building. Having a building is a blessing that God will often generously provide, but it should not be the main focus of a church.

13   As it is led to do so by the Holy Spirit, the body of believers in a local church can and should engage in giving to meet the needs of both local and international communities, but it should always do so with a spiritual end in mind, providing for material needs while pointing to the ultimate spiritual provision in Jesus Christ.

supplying for these physical needs, the churches that donated to the collection were also ministering in a spiritual way, strengthening the unity of believers.

While giving to your local church is a good way to minister to others through your finances, you can and should make disciples by giving to other ministry entities and organizations, as well as directly to specific individuals. As we mentioned earlier in this chapter, prayerfully seek the guidance of the Holy Spirit when considering where to give.

Whether you are an individual, a church leader, or part of a congregation wanting to give financially, take time to evaluate the potential ministries and organizations you are seeking to support. It is critical to ask if they are actually pursuing, promoting, and fulfilling the Great Commission by going into the world and spreading the good news of Jesus Christ. These organizations can vary greatly in terms of the people to whom they minister. Some care for the poor, needy, or helpless (perhaps providing food, shelter, or clothing); others focus on prisoners or the oppressed; still others pave the way for evangelism, preaching, and discipleship (such as through church planting or training pastors). When considering where to give, make sure you evaluate whether an organization is focusing solely on physical needs or whether an organization addresses both physical *and* spiritual needs. It is far better to give to a ministry that has Christ at its center than one that focuses only on the material world (for more on these categories, see the Appendix).

The following list[14] is a good place to start when discerning where to give. Consider whether the ministry:

- Has a goal of glorifying God and making disciples
- Is in accordance with sound biblical doctrine
- Fits your giving objectives and mission statement (if you have a spouse, make sure he or she is in line with this as well)

---

14   List adapted from Ronald Blue Trust resources.

- Has personal meaning for you and your family, or you know someone connected to it
- Employs leaders who are marked by godly characteristics
- Is growing and cooperative with others
- Is goal-oriented and active around the local community or the world
- Displays accountability and transparency in its business dealings
- Is innovative with dynamic approaches to solving problems
- Has a strong, measurable track record
- Is characterized by strong financial stewardship

When you give, prayerfully surrender your money to God and release your funds. You are simply a steward of what He already owns. It can be tempting to try to control exactly what happens with the finances we give—in our local church, for example, we may try to take control of leadership or service decisions when we donate a large sum of money—but this is not what God has called us to do. After we have researched and prayed over a ministry or given toward a specific cause, we need to release those funds and remember that they are in God's hands. Let it be His name that is glorified as we say along with John the Baptist, "He must increase, but I must decrease" (John 3:30).

PART TWO:

Practices of
Biblical Leverage

RUSS CROSSON

Now that we have built a solid foundation of the biblical principles of why, when, how, how much, and where to give, let's turn our attention to some best practices for how to apply these principles. It is one thing to *know* that we should do something, but it's quite another to actually follow through and *do* it.

How do we give according to our ability? Do we need a foundation to facilitate our giving? Where do our children factor into our giving? Should we consider our taxes when we determine our giving amount? Should we only give liquid assets, or should we consider giving other assets as well? What constitutes a good steward? Once you are ready to give, it is important to think through what that looks like for you, your family, and your estate. We will look at all of these issues in Part Two and give you the tools to help you answer these questions.

In order to truly leverage our temporal goods for eternal gain, we need to put the principles of giving into practice. Wisdom, after all, is the application of knowledge in a practical and successful way. As a financial advisor for over forty years, I have successfully used these giving methods over and over with individuals and couples. The next five chapters will help you use the knowledge in the first half of the book to apply specific practices to your generosity journey.

CHAPTER 6

The Importance of Accountability

As my friend Robert[15] stood to leave my office, I asked him, "So we agreed not to let your net worth increase any more, right?"

Robert and I had spent the last hour discussing giving according to his ability, wrestling with what he should leave to his children versus to charitable entities, looking at current versus deferred giving, and analyzing his financial finish line (all topics I will discuss in the

---

15   The names used throughout these chapters are pseudonyms.

upcoming chapters). We had settled on the fact that he had enough money to meet the needs of his family, and if God continued to increase his financial net worth, then he should consider giving that increase away as it grew and not waiting to leave it through his estate.

"Yes, that's what we decided," Robert responded somewhat forlornly.

"Well, let's see what God might do this year and how much you can increase your giving as you donate the growth of your net worth," I said as I shook his hand.

When Robert left my office that day, he knew I was going to hold him accountable to follow through on what he had concluded God wanted him to do—give away the increase of his net worth. He was willing to accept responsibility and accountability for his actions. He knew that at the end of the year, I would ask him if he had given away any increase in net worth. However, if I did not follow through, remind him, and hold him accountable, then it probably would not have happened. Why? Robert, like most of us, was not focused every day, or even every week, on giving assets away, and he needed accountability to remind him of his goals.

Robert's journey and follow-through were important if he was going to steward well the resources God had entrusted to him.

Stewardship

As we noted in chapter 1, God gives us wealth for several reasons and desires us to use it for His kingdom work. The key is to act on what we know. And we know that we are called to steward wisely what God has entrusted to us.

Christian financial author Ron Blue defines stewardship as the use of God-given resources for the accomplishment of God-given goals. The Merriam-Webster dictionary defines stewardship as the careful and responsible management of anything entrusted to our care. In combining these definitions, stewardship is managing everything God brings into our lives in a manner that honors Him. As we discussed in chapter 4, it's not the amount we have that matters, but rather what we *do* with what we have.

The classic parable of the talents found in Matthew 25:14–26 clearly shows this principle. The master leaves on a trip, but before he goes, he calls his servants together and entrusts his possessions to them. To one he leaves five talents, to another two talents, and to the final servant one talent—different amounts according to different abilities. When the master returns, he asks for an accounting of what happened to his possessions. The first two servants doubled what the master left to them, but the other just buried his one talent. The first two were praised and called faithful, while the third was chastised and called wicked and lazy. The first two servants showed their good stewardship through their purposeful investment of their master's funds, while the third servant demonstrated his lack of responsible management of the resources entrusted to him.

What Makes a Good Steward?

Am I a good steward if my investment account beats a certain investment index? Am I a bad steward if it does not? What if I keep money in the bank, earning very little interest—is that bad stewardship? Is having all of my assets invested in the stock market good stewardship? Is making an investment that loses money bad stewardship? What about purchasing a second home or buying new versus used cars? Shopping for clothes at Goodwill versus a boutique? Owning a boat or a motorcycle? What constitutes good stewardship?

If stewardship is the careful, responsible use of resources in a manner that honors God and accomplishes God-given goals, then one could make a case that any of the previous scenarios could illustrate either good or bad stewardship depending on the circumstances and motivation behind them. Let me demonstrate:

- If I keep cash on hand at a level that makes my spouse more comfortable, then my marriage harmony may trump the monetary return I'm giving up. On the other hand, I may keep cash on hand simply to hoard it for myself and keep it away from others.
- Perhaps buying better brands or higher-quality clothes or cars allows them to last longer and therefore I shop less often. On the other hand, I may purchase higher-end items to fit in or present a certain image.

- I may use my boat or second home for ministry, but on the other hand, I may own these things for my own luxury or to impress others.

One cannot conclude from these statements whether a financial choice is wise stewardship or not without context. So, how do you know if you are living as a good steward?

Good stewards engage in the process of financial decision-making based on biblical principles and allow themselves to be held accountable for the choices they make.

Good stewards engage in the process of financial decision-making based on biblical principles and allow themselves to be held accountable for the choices they make. Unless a financial decision violates the law or a clear biblical principle, then we are free to pray about whether to pursue it or not. We may wish the Bible gave us clear guidelines on how much to give, how much to save, how much to spend on a house, etc., but it doesn't. The financial decisions we make do not determine whether or not we are good stewards, but rather our engagement in this decision-making process does.

At the end of the day, we are responsible for stewarding what God has entrusted to us and for using it to bring honor to Him and accomplish His purposes. To achieve this, we need to mistrust ourselves. That's right—mistrust ourselves. We can convince ourselves of anything and therefore need instruction, a coach or guide, and accountability. The more wealth we have, the more critical this accountability becomes. We will all stand before God and make an account, and we all want to hear, *"Well done, good and faithful servant! You have been faithful with a few things; I will put you in charge of many things"* (Matthew 25:21 NIV). Only when we are face-to-face with our Creator will we know if we have lived as good stewards or not.

Submitting to God and seeking accountability as we engage in the financial decision-making process helps lead to peace of mind about our financial choices. Although we may not know our reward in heaven until we have completed our time on earth, we can strive to make wise financial decisions by knowing and practicing biblical financial principles; surrounding ourselves with wise counselors; and choosing like-minded financial professionals who can speak truth into our lives, help us see things from a new perspective, and hold us accountable for the way we deploy our finances.

What Is Financial Accountability?

Financial accountability is allowing someone into our lives who knows our complete financial situation and holds us responsible for our actions. Having this accountability increases the probability that we will live as wise stewards with everything that is entrusted to us.

Accountability can also help us overcome the subtle and potentially negative impact of wealth and money.

Accountability can also help us overcome the subtle and potentially negative impact of wealth and money. Known as the "Prince of Preachers," Charles Haddon Spurgeon said it this way: "It is a very serious thing to grow rich. Of all of the temptations to which God's children are exposed it is the worst, because it is the one that they do not dread, and therefore, it is the more subtle temptation."[16]

---

16 Charles Haddon Spurgeon, "Declension from First Love," Sermon on Revelation 2:4, New Park Street Chapel, Southwark, September 26, 1858.

Luke 16:13 states that we cannot serve two masters—God and money. In order to avoid serving money, we need to surrender our finances to God and put Him at the center of our lives. Giving as God leads is the only antidote to the temptation of accumulation that Spurgeon refers to. The more affluent we become, the more we need accountability to avoid serving money.

In the third century, Cyprian, the bishop of Carthage, wrote this description of the affluent:

> Their property held them in chains . . . chains which shackled their courage and choked their faith and hampered their judgment and throttled their soul. . . . If they stored up their treasure in heaven, they would not now have an enemy and a thief within their own household. . . . They think of themselves as owners, whereas it is they rather who are owned: enslaved as they are to their own property, they are not the masters of their money but its slaves.[17]

Cyprian says storing up treasures in heaven is the only way to avoid money as a master, and we do this partly by giving away our wealth. However, giving is not typically where we first use our resources. Therefore, accountability is necessary to move us toward a posture of generosity and maximize our giving.

What should you look for in an accountability partner? It is important to choose someone who has a good grasp on what the Bible says about money as well as the courage to challenge you to maximize your generosity during your lifetime and not only after your death.

Sometimes, a like-minded Christian will meet these qualifications. However, they may not have expertise with charitable-giving vehicles and techniques that a professional advisor can provide. Therefore, you may need to enlist a like-minded financial professional

---

17   Cyprian, *Treatise III: On the Lapsed.*

as well. Fortunately, the Christian financial industry has grown, and these individuals are more accessible than ever.[18]

As you work through this book, our hope is that the directive, "to whom much was given, of him much will be required" (Luke 12:48b), will challenge you, and you will allow someone to hold you accountable for what God has entrusted to you.

---

18 Ronald Blue Trust has offered biblically based financial advice since 1979. Its mission is to assist Christians in fulfilling the Great Commission through generosity. In the early 2000s the Ronald Blue Trust methodology and biblically based advice model was expanded through a group of advisors called Kingdom Advisors.

CHAPTER 7

Current Versus Deferred Giving

Most tables were full, but I found one that had an empty seat. There are only a few places where one can sit under the stars and have a meal free from bugs or humidity, but Tucson, Arizona, in late April is one of those places. I was attending a ministry event with donors from all over the country who had gathered to celebrate the ministry's impact around the country and the world.

As we introduced ourselves at the table, we settled into conversations about generosity and helping the ministry. The individuals at my table took turns sharing why they were involved in the ministry and, to my surprise, were quite forthright about what they were planning to donate to the ministry in the future. The couple to my right shared that they were planning to leave a large amount to the ministry through their estate. I listened intently and then offered the idea that maybe they could give that money now instead of later. Why wait?

That suggestion stopped the easy dialogue cold. They all looked at me like I had two heads. I proposed that if people are planning to give money to a ministry upon their death, then they should at least entertain the idea of giving it now instead.

Needless to say, the rest of the evening's discussions revolved around why I had made that recommendation. I shared reasons why people are hesitant to give currently, and I explained the benefits of giving now versus through a will or estate. I heard later that the couple was seriously considering my challenge.

Before we dive into the reasons someone might consider giving now as opposed to later, let's define the terms current giving and deferred giving.

Current and Deferred Giving

For our discussion, *current giving* is any gift donated while you are alive (with a warm hand) in the form of cash, assets, business interests, real estate, etc.

In contrast, *deferred giving* is any gift donated after your death (with a cold hand)—cash, assets, business interests, real estate, etc.—through your will or estate. It does not include donations that you defer to a later date or over time, such as a three-year pledge to a charity. That giving is simply the delayed timing of a current gift.

As you consider current versus deferred giving, you should ask yourself the following questions:

1. What would I do with my wealth if I knew I was going to die in twelve months?
2. What would I do with my wealth if I knew the Lord would return in twelve months?

At first glance, these questions may appear the same. But are they? The first question necessitates some planning. It requires you to go through the process of determining your financial finish line (the finite amount that is enough for you), how much wealth you need to provide for your family, how much money you can give, and where you will give your assets.

However, the second question is quite different. The answer to that question is (hopefully) that you don't want to hoard a pile of assets instead of investing them in what matters for eternity. Are you traveling light? Have you only kept what you need for your short time on this earth? Are you gaining eternal reward with your excess assets and financial resources by investing in the work of God during your lifetime?

Since we do not know when we will leave this earth or when the Lord will return, we need to live with both scenarios in mind, which means continually maximizing planning and generosity, both currently and through our wills.[19]

Hesitancy about Current Giving

In his book *The Treasure Principle*, Randy Alcorn uses the following analogy:

> Imagine you were alive at the end of the Civil War. You're living in the South, but you are a Northerner. You plan to move home as soon as the war is over. While in the South you've accumulated lots of Confederate currency. Now, suppose you know for a fact the North is going to win the war soon. What will you do with your Confederate money? If you're smart, you'll immediately cash in your excess Confederate currency for US currency—the only money that will have value after the war. You'll keep only enough Confederate currency to meet your short-term needs.[20]

19 Although this chapter focuses primarily on current giving, it is wise to have a will that clearly states your testamentary desires, including charitable giving.

20 Randy Alcorn, *The Treasure Principle: Unlocking the Secret of Joyful Giving* (New York: Multnomah Publishers, 2017), 7.

Since earth is not our long-term, eternal home, we should store up treasures in heaven and not here on earth (Matthew 6:19–20). So why are people hesitant to give now? There are many reasons, but the following are some of the most common concerns.

Since earth is not our long-term, eternal home, we should store up treasures in heaven and not here on earth (Matthew 6:19–20).

---

1. Fear. People are often afraid they may not have enough if they give away wealth now. The most common reason for hesitancy with current giving is the fear of the "what ifs": What if I get sick? What if I lose my job? What if my spouse loses his or her job? What if I need to take care of my parents? What if the stock market crashes? What if inflation gets out of hand? What if my children need something that I can't afford?

The list of "what ifs" is endless, and the way to counter it is through trust in God and accountability (review chapter 1 on God's provision). We need someone in our lives who will challenge us to at least ask the question, "Why not give it away now?" It is okay to have fears, and courageous to admit them. The key is to remain teachable and open. Consider giving at a level that takes you out of your comfort zone (see the "Give Sacrificially" section in chapter 4). It is a leap of faith, but the reward will be great, and God promises to always meet our needs (Philippians 4:19). Spirit-led generosity helps us to define ourselves by who and whose we are rather than by our earthly wealth.

For example, think back to the client I mentioned in the preface at the beginning of the book. He had many fears about giving away too much, but he was teachable. He considered suggestions for current giving that took him beyond his comfort level, and he gave more than he had donated historically. He took a step of faith and gave the asset or wrote out the check. He gave while he was alive—with a warm hand.

When he died, his reward was great—he had an impact on countless lives on earth and stored up incredible treasures in heaven.

2. Limited Liquid Assets. Sometimes people do not give during their lifetime because they have limited cash or liquid assets. Instead, they have non-liquid assets like real estate, partnerships, or business interests, which are not as simple to gift and, in many cases, require sophisticated tax planning. As a result of the complexity, people often conclude it is easier to donate assets through their will rather than now. One of the biggest drawbacks to this thinking is that people miss out on rewards in heaven and kingdom impact today. We are rewarded for what we do "while in the body," not after we die. Second Corinthians 5:9–10 says, "So we make it our goal to please him, whether we are at home in the body or away from it. For we must all appear before the judgment seat of Christ, so that *each of us may receive what is due us for the things done while in the body*, whether good or bad" (NIV; emphasis added).

In his book *The Law of Rewards,* Randy Alcorn makes this point as well:

> Hebrews 9:27 says, "It is appointed for men to die once, but after this the judgment" (NKJV). We will be rewarded for what we actually do on earth. I think that leaving instructions for what others are to do with what we leave behind is not the same as what we do while we're still alive.

> Would Jesus have pointed to the woman who gave away her last two coins in the same way if she had died that day and left those same two coins to the temple charity in her will? I don't think so. Would he be pleased that she left the coins in her will, as opposed to wasting them? Sure. But I don't think the reward would be comparable.

I think God rewards faith and sacrifice. It takes no faith or sacrifice to leave stuff behind when you die, since hanging on to it is not an alternative. Giving is choosing to part with something, while leaving is simply controlling the destination of what you couldn't hold on to.

Now, we will all leave something behind, and certainly it is good to leave substantial portions to the church and to Christian ministries. I simply don't think we should consider this a substitute for true giving, which is done while we are still alive and when we still must trust God to provide.[21]

As we discussed in chapter 4, it is not necessarily the amount one gives that matters. Instead, it is the giver's heart of sacrificial obedience and the recognition that we are stewards and ambassadors of God, the owner of all things. If you need help with how to give when you have limited liquid assets, you can consult a financial advisor for assistance with giving now in addition to giving through your will.

3. Not Understanding God's Command to Give. Not giving generously during our lifetime may reveal a *poor understanding of the reasons WHY we give* (see chapter 1). We always follow through on what is important to us—what we perceive as valuable and advantageous to us. Limited current giving could indicate that some of the reasons we give—such as meeting the needs of others, giving as a form of worship, giving out of obedience to God, storing up treasures in heaven, acknowledging God's ownership, and breaking the power of money in our lives—are not priorities for us. If the desire for comfort and luxury outweighs our obedience to live generously, then we need to reexamine our priorities.

---

21 Randy Alcorn, *The Law of Rewards: Giving What You Can't Keep to Gain What You Can't Lose* (Carol Stream, IL: Tyndale House, 2003).

4. Failure to Have a Plan. Sometimes people do not give currently because they don't realize they *can* give now, don't know *how* to give now, or don't have a *plan* to give now. For example, a person with minimal cash or liquid investments may not realize they can give a non-liquid asset. I have seen this time and time again. People think they can only give cash and do not know they can donate a piece of their business, real estate, stocks, or mutual funds. Once they are aware they can give a non-liquid asset, then they may need help with how to gift it. The donation also needs to work within their overall financial plan. It is important for them to see that they can give now and still meet their needs and goals—put food on the table, educate their children, and reach their financial goals.

5. Not Understanding the Benefits. Finally, current giving is often not part of people's plan because they do not understand its benefits. In my experience, once people begin to understand the benefits, they become more open to giving now versus later.

Benefits of Current Versus Deferred Giving

Because our natural tendency is to focus on what we lose rather than on what we gain when we give, let's take a closer look at some of the benefits of current giving.

1. Current giving allows the giver to experience the joy of giving, see the money working now, and start heavenly compounding.

Experience the Joy of Giving: Although we do receive treasure in heaven for giving now, we also receive earthly benefits. One of those benefits is joy, particularly because of the fellowship we have with other believers when we give to them. Paul writes in 1 Thessalonians 2:19–20: "For what is our hope, our joy, or the crown in which we will glory in the presence of our Lord Jesus when he comes? Is it not you? Indeed, you are our glory and joy" (NIV).

See the Money Working Now: Current giving also allows us to see the outcome of our giving. Sometimes we think we should grow our assets first and then give more later. The fallacy with that plan is twofold. First, what if, like the rich fool in Luke 12, our soul is taken tonight? We aren't guaranteed tomorrow to give generously. Second, what investment return have we given up if we wait to give?

Let's use the Rule of 72 to illustrate what you may have given up by waiting to give.[22] Using this rule, if you have $100,000 to invest and earn 6 percent on your investments, then the money would grow to $200,000 in twelve years. You have doubled your money and have $200,000 to give away, but you have to wait twelve years. However, what if you invested the $100,000 today in the following ways?

- Distribute 1,000 Bibles: $5,000
- Drill 20 wells for clean drinking water: $30,000
- Train 200 pastors: $15,000
- Fund evangelism ministry that produces 2,000 new Christians: $20,000
- Fund a marriage ministry that has an impact on 1,000 marriages: $15,000
- Provide meals and job training for 200 homeless people: $5,000
- Provide discipleship materials for university students: $10,000

By the time you would have given the $200,000 twelve years from now, your $100,000 gift has already had numerous benefits. How many pastors trained; new Christians, mature Christians, and college students grounded in their faith; families rescued out of poverty; and marriages saved? You were also able to experience and see the impact of your generosity.

Put another way, how much kingdom impact was lost by not giving $100,000 when you could? We are not guaranteed to experience and see these impacts, but that is not why we give. We never know how much God is at work behind the scenes. Perhaps no one was saved through our financial generosity (at least, not that we witness),

---

22 The Rule of 72 tells you how long it takes to double your money. Divide seventy-two by your rate of return to determine the amount of time it takes to double your money.

but we may simply be paving the way for others. Sowing seeds now may result in reaping a harvest much, much later.

Start Heavenly Compounding: The investment principle of compounding says one dollar invested today is worth multiple dollars in the future. However, the Bible suggests a second compounding principle: **reverse compounding**. Our compounding period is unknown but declining every day as we continue to age. The resulting math is as clear as it is sobering: *the future value of our giving declines each day as our time on earth lessens.* One dollar given today is worth more than one dollar given tomorrow because money given sooner has more time to compound for the recipient as well as for the future rewards of the giver (Philippians 4:17, Matthew 6:19–20). Jesus was keenly aware that the compounding period shortens every day: "We must work the works of Him who sent Me as long as it is day; night is coming when no one can work" (John 9:4 NASB).

Our compounding period is unknown but declining every day as we continue to age.

For Christians who delay giving, the principle of reverse compounding works against them twice—in this life and in the life to come. While we know Jesus commands us to lay up treasure in heaven (Matthew 6:20), we often overlook the fact that the sooner we do this, the longer He has to compound that treasure for His glory and our good. No one is suggesting financial irresponsibility in this world, but waiting to give doesn't make sense—eternally or mathematically. Some people think, "When a stock hits a certain number, I will give," or "I can invest my money wisely myself, then I will give," or "I will give when I die." To hold on to your wealth implies you can invest better than God, or you prefer earthly compounding versus eternal compounding. To wait to give says you have projected the metrics of the world onto the metrics of the kingdom, thinking you can quantify the return.

God is not limited by the power of compounding, but He invites us to participate in His work by giving now rather than later. Although His grace is sufficient to overcome any difference that may result from us waiting to give, presuming on His goodness and grace is unwise. Since we are not guaranteed tomorrow, the sooner we start giving, the more we maximize our compounding period. If you are feeling reluctant to give, ask the Spirit to work in your heart, review the many blessings God has given you, and try to emulate Christ-like generosity for others.

2. Current giving encourages and provides an opportunity to live by faith.

How do we live by faith? We are told that "faith is the assurance of things hoped for, the conviction of things not seen" (Hebrews 11:1 NASB). When many of us began our careers, we were living by faith because we weren't sure how our income and expenses would balance out month to month. However, we trusted that God would meet our needs (Philippians 4:19), and we walked by faith. We prayed fervently and lived in the confident assurance of God's promise to provide for us.

However, as our lives moved along, many of us began to accumulate more and have a surplus of financial resources in the bank or retirement or both. As this happened, it was easy to take our focus from God and move it to our "pile" of wealth. Our security and faith slowly drifted from God to our pile. Giving now helps us return our faith and trust to God instead of trusting in the pile we have accumulated. If we are consistently giving now, then it forces us to deal with tradeoffs, make lifestyle decisions, and sacrifice.

One year my wife suggested we give a rather large sum of money to a ministry she was involved with. I asked, "Where is that money going to come from?" She sweetly responded, "From that pile we have in the bank." I hadn't even considered that money. I felt it was there accumulating for a reason. However, we gave the gift, reduced the size of our pile, and experienced a good reminder that without a continued focus on giving currently, it is easy to allow our piles to grow and inadvertently put our faith there.

It is not enough to plan to give large amounts later if we haven't considered what we are called to do and can afford to give now. If our desire for comfort or security comes before a desire to give sacrificially and see God's will done today, then we need to reexamine our lives and consider giving more as a reminder that God owns it all. We are merely stewards and ambassadors for the funds with which He has provided us.

3. Current giving breaks the power of money in our lives.

Giving now helps us open our hands and break the power of money in our lives (Luke 16:11–13). The more material wealth we have, the more gravitational force that wealth exerts on us. It pulls us into its orbit. Ecclesiastes 5:13 says, "I have seen a grievous evil under the sun: wealth hoarded to the harm of its owners" (NIV). This truth may be the greatest benefit of current giving—it provides an escape from the insidious pull of money on our lives as we limit its growth.

_____

Giving now helps us open our hands and break the power of money in our lives.

_____

The more wealth we have, the more time it takes to evaluate it, manage it, and protect it. In other words, we begin spending more time thinking about our finances and less time concerned with eternal things. We may use a second home or boat wisely, but each addition to the pile increases the pull of material things in our lives. In Acts 28:30–31, Paul said he was living in rented quarters and was able to preach openly and without being hindered by a large amount of material goods. He did not own much; he traveled light.

Each of us must wrestle with how much wealth is too much or enough for us by surrendering our finances to God and praying and asking the Spirit to guide us. The Bible does not provide a formula for how to live financially and how much to accumulate, but we know that money can distract us from God's guidance. We also know that Scripture (see Proverbs 25:16 and Exodus 16:16–20) cautions us against excess, which can be defined as beyond the common measure or proportion, extreme, overindulgent, extravagant, wasteful. Current giving can provide an antidote to excess.

Luke 16:11–13 says we cannot serve God and money. Only one can be on the throne of our hearts. Current giving helps keep God on the throne instead of money, which constantly strives to ascend the throne.

4. Current giving allows us to take advantage of the government matching program.

Although this benefit of current giving is practical in nature rather than theological, and it may not apply in every country, it should still have an impact on our decision to give now rather than later. In the United States, for every dollar we give (either cash or assets), we can deduct a dollar on our tax return. The government is in essence returning it to us via a tax refund of 20 to 30 percent (the exact amount is dependent on our effective tax rate). As long as the tax laws allow a deduction for charitable giving, it makes sense to give now and allow the government to supplement some of our giving. Giving more now while we are alive may also help our heirs avoid potential estate tax in the future.

Although we all have calendars with 365 days, we should live with only two days circled—today and Judgment Day (the day we stand before the Lord and make an account of what He has entrusted to us). Yesterday is gone, and we can't count on tomorrow. I encourage you to live wisely today. Be open to giving your money, assets, and other resources away as fast as they come in. Take God up on His challenge in Malachi 3:10: "'Bring the whole tithe into the storehouse, that there may be food in my house. Test me in this,' says the Lord Almighty, 'and see if I will not throw open the floodgates of heaven and pour out so much blessing that there will not be room enough to store it'" (NIV). This principle is the same in the New Testament: "You will be enriched in every way so that you can be generous on every occasion, and through us your generosity will result in thanksgiving to God" (2 Corinthians 9:11 NIV). In my forty-plus years of helping people live generously, I have found it is impossible to out-give God.

CHAPTER 8

Cash Flow Versus Net Worth Giving

As I sat down at the table to meet my longtime friend and client Steve, I could not help but reflect on our relationship over the years. Steve first came to my office when I was very new in the business, and he was in a similar place in his career. He had joined the family business, did not have much income, and had been encouraged by a mentor to get financial planning advice as he and his wife, Sarah, were in the early stages of building their family and business.

When we began meeting, I would help Steve and Sarah make sure they were on track to accomplish their financial goals—providing for their children's education, getting out of debt, ensuring they had adequate life insurance, and having enough money to retire. We would also check to see that they were giving generously. As time passed and their business prospered, our discussions focused more on charitable giving. I had challenged them to begin grappling with questions like, "How much is enough?", "How much can we give?", and "How much do we really need?"

Now, as Steve joined me at the table, I asked, "Do you remember the time I challenged you to consider giving six figures to charity in one year?"

"Do I remember?! How could I forget? I thought you were crazy!" Steve said as he laughed. "I thought for sure I would go broke doing something like that."

"But that didn't happen, did it?" I inquired with a smile.

"No, it did not," he replied. "It really is true . . . you can't out-give God."

Steve and I were meeting because he was not only continuing to wrestle with the question of how much to give, but now he was also trying to determine his financial finish line and answer the question, "How much is enough?" From a financial standpoint, there are two places to look to help determine how much we can give and how much is enough. One is our cash flow giving, and the other is our net worth giving. Many people are only aware of their cash flow giving.

Cash Flow Giving

Let's take a closer look at cash flow giving based on Figure 8.1.

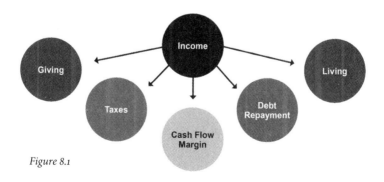

Figure 8.1

Income is money from a salary, bonuses, dividends, interest, rental income, investment income, partnership income, corporate distributions, etc. In short, it is simply a total of all the money you receive from any source, and it is usually any money you pay taxes on. However, income does not include cash gifts or tax refunds.

Everything you do with money fits in one of five categories: giving, taxes, debt, living expenses, and savings. **Giving** includes any money (cash, credit card, check) given to a deductible charity, a 501(c)(3) organization (e.g., a church, ministry, or nonprofit organization), plus any amount given to a nondeductible entity (e.g., family, friends, neighbors). This category does not include gifts for birthdays, anniversaries, or Christmas, which are part of living expenses. **Income taxes** are your total amount of federal, state, Medicare, and Social Security taxes. **Debt** is the amount you owe on credit cards, student loans, car loans, etc. Debt does not include your home mortgage, which is included in living expenses. **Living expenses** are what you spend to live—utilities, groceries, vacations, car insurance, gifts, clothing, medical expenses, home mortgage, etc. **Savings** refers to the amount left after subtracting giving, taxes, debt, and living expenses from income.

Cash flow is simply allocating your received income into the five categories shown in Figure 8.1, one of which is giving. When most people determine their giving amount, they simply calculate a percentage of their income. The resulting number (income multiplied by giving percentage) is what we would call "cash flow giving." Figure 8.2 shows a sample income for David of $100,000 with 10 percent, or $10,000, given annually.

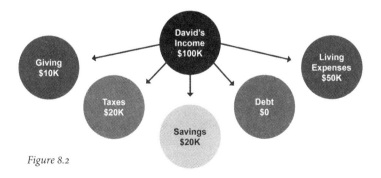

Figure 8.2

David is tithing out of their cash flow. What else could he do? He can't give what he doesn't have, correct? While that is true (we discussed Paul's admonition to give out of what we have in chapter 4), the problem in this illustration is that David has not considered a second factor—his net worth.

Net Worth Giving

Net worth is a summary of every financial decision a person has ever made. A list of assets and liabilities captures someone's current net worth. Why does net worth matter? In the simplest of terms, net worth is important because it affects one's overall financial picture. Most people have investment accounts that increase in value over time. Table 8.1 illustrates this principle for David.

Table 8.1: David's Net Worth		
Cash	$150K	
Investments	$600K at 5%	= $30K
Retirement	$500K at 5% + $25K	= $50K
Business	$1,500K at 6%	= $90K
Home	$500K	
TOTAL	$2,750K	$170K

David has cash, investments, retirement, a business, and a home. He also has no liabilities or debt. In Table 8.1, we have assumed a 5 percent growth rate on David's investments, which in this example equals an increase of $30,000.

Many investors also have retirement accounts, which typically grow organically in a similar manner to investment accounts each year. However, retirement accounts usually increase more quickly because people continue to fund them on a regular basis. Table 8.1 shows a 5 percent growth in David's retirement account plus an annual contribution of $25,000.

Usually, business owners take a salary from their business (this appears as cash in Table 8.1) and distributions for taxes (which is also accounted for as cash in our example). However, significant earnings are often left in the business, which allows the business value to increase. In addition, as the business grows, its inherent value may also increase. For our illustration, we have assumed a 6 percent growth rate in David's business, which is a conservative assumption.

The punch line is that David had an increase of $170,000 in his net worth growth (see Table 8.1), but that is not the only growth. Looking back at Figure 8.2, you will see that he has $20,000 in savings. If you add this amount to the current cash balance of $150,000, then it increases David's net worth by $20,000. So, in total, his net worth increased $190,000 year-over-year.

Although your numbers may look different than this example, the concept of net worth growth still holds true.

Considerations for Net Worth Giving

Several factors will influence whether you should consider giving from your net worth, including your age, career timeline, and current financial situation. When you begin your career and are working to build a business, sharpen your skills, pay off debt, start funding retirement, and save for education, then most of your giving will come from your cash flow. However, as you move through your career and your net worth continues to grow, you should expand your focus to also include your net worth when considering how much to give.

To avoid becoming like the rich fool in Luke 12 by just building bigger barns, you will need to ask some difficult and poignant questions, like: *Why am I allowing my net worth to grow? Do I need it to increase at this rate? Do I have a future use for this growth?* If you do not have obvious answers to these questions, then most likely you are approaching your financial finish line and have already answered the question, "How much is enough?" and you should consider what else you can do with your wealth.

Some people have a smaller income and net worth and may never reach the point of giving from their net worth, and that is okay. We are called to give according to our ability. So, the most important act of financial obedience is giving what God leads us to give and not allowing our pile to continue to grow without a purpose. Perhaps we are saving for education, retirement, etc., but we also need to consider if we can give more than we thought we could out of our net worth.

Pulling the Factors Together

To answer the question *How much should I give?*, start by looking at both cash flow and net worth and ask: *Are there any reasons not to give the maximum amount the government allows me to deduct on my income taxes?* Why ask this question? The government is essentially "matching" your charitable contribution at your effective tax rate (the percentage of your taxable income that you pay in taxes). For example, if you have an effective tax rate of 20 percent and give $10,000, you get a tax refund of $2,000 so the gift only "costs" you $8,000.[23] Instead of giving merely $10,000, you probably have the financial ability to give $12,000.

In Figure 8.2, David earned $100,000 per year. Current tax laws would allow him to give $60,000 and deduct it all. Can he "afford" to give this much? Of course he can! His net worth increase for the year was $190,000, so if he donated an additional $50,000, then his net worth would still grow by $140,000. This growth does not even include any charitable tax savings from the deduction.

While the tax savings on our donations are appealing and beneficial, our main reason for giving should not be the tax refund we will receive. As we mentioned earlier, giving demonstrates obedience to God's commands, acknowledges His ownership of everything, allows us to participate in His work while on earth, shows gratitude, and includes the promise of future eternal rewards.

My friend, Steve, and his wife, whom I mentioned earlier in this chapter, give generously (about $300,000 a year), which is six times what they were planning to give from their cash flow, and yet their net worth still continues to grow. They reached this level of generosity because they grappled with the "how much to give"

---

23 Tax laws change frequently. Be sure to check current laws or consult a Certified Public Accountant (CPA).

question and factored in both their net worth and their cash flow when determining the answer.

To give according to our ability, we must take into account our cash flow *and* net worth. If we can give the maximum amount that we can deduct for taxes, then we should consider giving that amount, if not more. Not because of the tax benefit, but because that is wise stewardship that will move us closer to giving according to our ability as discussed in chapter 4.

———————

To give according to our ability, we must take into account our cash flow and *net worth.*

———————

Complicating Factors of How to Give

After we decide the amount to give, it is important to figure out *how* to give it. Should we only give cash, or should we donate other assets, such as publicly traded stock, real estate, or business interests? It is my experience that if we give according to how we have been blessed, asset giving is part of the answer to the "how" question

As we mentioned earlier, business owners may have a particularly difficult time giving as they have been blessed. They usually have marginal cash and minimal liquidity. They can often earn more money with assets invested in the business than they can by moving them to cash. The better a business performs, the more potential the owner has to give generously, but he or she may need to consider giving business stock or other assets rather than cash.

This conundrum is what my friend, Steve, and I were processing that day at lunch. We were looking at his cash flow and net worth for the year. His income had increased, his investment account had grown dramatically, and so had his retirement plan.

Hesitantly he asked, "You are probably going to tell me I can give away all I earned this year, right? It seems like just yesterday we were trying to figure out how to give a tithe."

I smiled and said, "You have been blessed, my friend. I can only show you the numbers and remind you of your finish line. Then it is between you and the Lord to determine what you do next. But to answer your question, yes, you can give away all you earned last year, and your net worth will not decrease."

As Steve finished his meal, he said, "I figured as much. Let me know the best way to give the assets. Thanks for your help. I always appreciate your honesty and keen insights."

We are called to give according to our ability and not just continue to grow our pile, which is why it's important to look at both cash flow and net worth when determining how much to give. Second Corinthians 8:12–14 reminds us that we are not called to give so that we suffer through our lack, but rather so that we meet needs out of our joy in Christ. As we age and our net worth grows, the amount we can give typically increases as well.

CHAPTER 9

Finding the Finish Line

I have worked with couples and individuals for over forty years and found that, while everyone's financial situation is different, many people experience similar issues. Roger and Alice were coming into our office to determine whether or not our firm could help them with their finances. They wanted to make sure they were living as good stewards of all God had entrusted to them. As I introduced myself, I couldn't help but notice that although they were both in their early to mid-70s, they were in great health, impeccably dressed, and did not look their ages. As we walked back to my office, I wondered about their story. What circumstances caused them to reach out for this meeting? What questions were they hoping I could help answer?

As we settled in, Roger shared that he and Alice had started a business right out of college and then mortgaged their home and everything they owned several times in the early years to keep it going. Through hard work and God's blessings, the business prospered and was still going strong. The success of the business allowed them to experience more financial success than they had ever dreamed possible. They were thrilled that their four adult children were involved in the business, but as the business risks had grown over the past few years, Roger and Alice wondered if their children would ever really have it as good as they did.

They also mentioned that they enjoyed travelling and spending time with their grandchildren. They hoped to fund part of the grandkids' college education and leave a respectable inheritance to their children. They went on to share that they enjoyed giving generously and were especially fond of their state university, which had named a couple of buildings after them. However, they weren't sure if they could continue to give generously and still have enough to live.

They had brought their personal balance sheet and most recent income tax return with them, as I had requested. These two pieces of information would help me create a picture of their financial situation and from there give them direction on how to accomplish their goals, answer their concerns, and hopefully achieve financial peace of mind.

As Roger pushed the documents across the table to me, I noticed that one listed his assets and liabilities and the other her assets and liabilities. I quickly glanced down at the assets he listed and the values beside each one—home, business, real estate, second home, stock portfolios, etc. He had no debt. The total at the bottom of the page was $123,000. I glanced at Alice's balance sheet. Similar assets were listed, and the total at the bottom of her page was $83,000.

I was somewhat surprised. Given all they had told me about the success of the business, I assumed that their net worth (the value of their assets minus their liabilities) would be higher than $206,000. Then I looked more closely at the bottom of the documents. In fine print it said, "Numbers rounded to the nearest thousand." Wow! They actually had over $200 million, not $200,000. And you know what? They still had the same question that so many others have: *Do we have enough to continue giving generously and still maintain our current lifestyle?*

Although this is the question many people ask, it is not really the best question to ask. As we discussed in chapter 4, God may call us to change our current lifestyle by giving up or sacrificing something we currently have or enjoy. That doesn't mean we won't have enough to meet our needs, but it may mean that we don't live at the same level we are used to living. The key is to be open to sacrifice and not tied to our current lifestyle.

The key is to be open to sacrifice and not tied to our current lifestyle.

Now, before you have the same thought I did ("Of course $200 million is enough"), let me share a couple of insights. First, we need to answer the question, "How much is enough?"—also known as a financial finish line—or we will continue to accumulate more. Without a God-centered mindset, there is never enough (Ecclesiastes 5:10). Second, the answer is different for everyone and may change over time. However, everyone should know their unique finish line number—the financial amount that is enough for them to meet their needs. Otherwise, they will always want or feel they need more.

The rich fool in Luke 12 is a classic example of someone who sought satisfaction in riches instead of God and did not answer the question, "How much is enough?" Let's pick up the story at Luke 12:17:

He began reasoning to himself, saying, "What shall I do, since I have no place to store my crops?" Then he said, "This is what I will do: I will tear down my barns and build larger ones, and there I will store all my grain and my goods. And I will say to my soul, 'Soul, you have many goods laid up for many years to come; take your ease, eat, drink and be merry.'"

(vv. 17–19 NASB)

That plan did not work out well for the rich fool—that night he died, and all he had accumulated was left to someone else. In addition, since he was not rich toward God (Luke 12:21), he was called a fool. Being rich toward God is using financial resources to meet needs and advance His kingdom, and to do good and be rich in good works (1 Timothy 6:17–19).

Unfortunately, this illustration is repeated by many people today—they don't prayerfully set their financial finish line, so they keep building larger piles, bigger barns, and higher net worth. Without a finish line, people may not live as generously as they could if they knew they had enough to meet their needs, and we all have enough because God promises to meet our needs (Matthew 6:25–34; Psalm 37:25). If people are not open to the giving opportunities that God puts before them or that stretch them, then they may always believe they need just a little bit more and therefore never get around to maximizing their giving. My fear for them, as for the rich fool, is found in James 5:1–3 (NASB):

Come now, you rich, weep and howl for your miseries which are coming upon you. Your riches have rotted and your garments have become moth-eaten. Your gold and your silver have rusted; and their rust will be a witness against you and will consume your flesh like fire. It is in the last days that you have stored up your treasure!

What the rich fool left was a witness to his greed. I don't want that to be my legacy or yours.

The book *Die Broke* by Stephen Pollan gives an interesting perspective on how to live and how to die. It expands on the idea of dying broke and makes a case that the last check we write should go to the funeral home. We came into this world with nothing, and we will leave with nothing. Ecclesiastes 5:15 says, "As he had come naked from his mother's womb, so will he return as he came. He will take nothing from the fruit of his labor that he can carry in his hand" (NASB).

John Wesley, the well-known English preacher and founder of the Methodist church, had a similar perspective on finish lines. During his life, he was one of the wealthiest men in England. In his day, when someone could live on 30 pounds per year, he made 1,400 pounds. Wesley was afraid of laying up treasures on earth, so he sent his money out to charity as quickly as it came in. In 1744 he wrote, "When I die if I leave behind me ten pounds . . . you and all mankind can bear witness against me, that I have lived and died a thief and a robber."[24] When he died in 1791, the only money mentioned in his will was the miscellaneous coins in his pockets and dresser drawers. Most of the 30,000 pounds (equivalent to $30 million today) he had earned in his lifetime had been given away.

This altruism *sounds* good, but executing it is where the difficulty arises. We are not necessarily called to die broke, leave what John Wesley left, or consider ourselves thieves and robbers if we leave behind ten pounds or more. Since we do not know the exact date of our death, it is nearly impossible to accomplish these standards. The goal is to give generously and not keep excess for our own benefit or safeguard (Proverbs 25:16). Rather, we are to provide for our families (1 Timothy 5:8), leave an inheritance to our children's children (Proverbs 13:22), and give generously (Deuteronomy 16:17).

---

24   Charles Edward White, "Four Lessons on Money," Christian History Institute, accessed July 12, 2022, https://christianhistoryinstitute.org/magazine/article/four-lessons-on-money.

We often worry about what expenses may occur in the future—children's education, long-term care, caring for loved ones, etc. With all these unknowns, is it even possible to determine a finish line? The answer is yes, it is possible. Let's look at the variables that go into finding the answer.

————————

The goal is to give generously and not keep excess for our own benefit or safeguard.

————————

Variables to Determine Your Finish Line

The following diagram (Figure 9.1) shows the variables to consider when determining your finish line: age, income, living expenses, giving percentage, projected investment return, inflation rate, retirement funding (if applicable), and federal and state effective tax rates.[25] In this example, Sam is age 60 and has an annual income of $430,000. He and his wife, Donna, give 10 percent of their income. The graph at the bottom of the figure shows that Sam does not run out of money with the assumed variables and still has investable assets of approximately $1.5 million at age 100.

Figure 9.2 illustrates the impact on Sam's finish line if some of the variable assumptions change. For instance, if he retires at age 70 instead of 65, increases his living expenses by 5 percent, and expands his giving, he still has enough assets to last until age 100.

————————

25 Financial planning software can show all possible variables. This diagram only shows the critical variables to determine this individual's finish line. Other variables could include education numbers, income for the spouse, etc., depending on the unique situation of the person.

CURRENT PLAN - SAM RETIRES AT AGE 65; 10% GIVING; LIVING EXPENSES OF $167K

Assumptions

Income		Assets	Balance	Growth Rate
Sam	430,000	Cash	178,807	1.0%
Donna	-	Liquid	2,671,509	5.9%
		Education	-	
Expenses		Non Liquid	174,959	3.0%
Living	167,340	Retirement	1,347,351	6.0%
Other	150,000	Business	1,050	
Giving		Personal	1,548,000	0.3%
% of Income	10%	Total Assets	5,921,676	4.2%

Retirement Contributions		Liabilities	
Employee	68,000	Personal	102,108
Employer	-	Business	-
		Total Liabilities	102,108

General	
Inflation Rate	3.0%
Retirement Age - Sam	65
Retirement Age - Donna	65
Federal Tax Rate- effective	15.1%
State Tax Rate - effective	4.0%

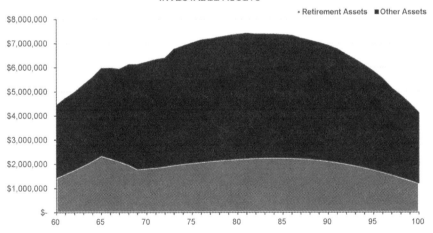

INVESTABLE ASSETS

- Retirement Assets ■ Other Assets

Figure 9.1

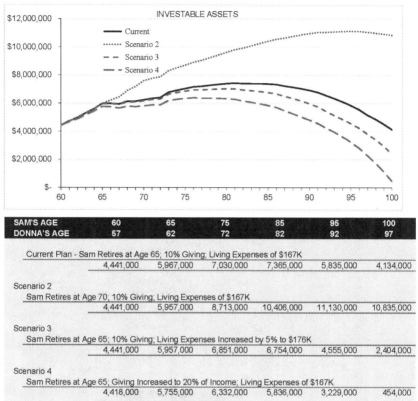

SAM'S AGE	60	65	75	85	95	100
DONNA'S AGE	57	62	72	82	92	97

Current Plan - Sam Retires at Age 65; 10% Giving; Living Expenses of $167K

	4,441,000	5,967,000	7,030,000	7,365,000	5,835,000	4,134,000

Scenario 2
Sam Retires at Age 70; 10% Giving; Living Expenses of $167K

	4,441,000	5,957,000	8,713,000	10,406,000	11,130,000	10,835,000

Scenario 3
Sam Retires at Age 65; 10% Giving; Living Expenses Increased by 5% to $176K

	4,441,000	5,957,000	6,851,000	6,754,000	4,555,000	2,404,000

Scenario 4
Sam Retires at Age 65; Giving Increased to 20% of Income; Living Expenses of $167K

	4,418,000	5,755,000	6,332,000	5,836,000	3,229,000	454,000

The balances shown are the total investable assets at the end of the year for the client's age.

Figure 9.2

Figures 9.1 and 9.2 provide an illustration for people considering their finish line to address common worries and "what if" scenarios that are often at the forefront of their thinking. Some of these concerns may include:

- What if I go into an assisted living home?
- What if tax brackets go up?
- What if my investment return is less than projected?
- What if inflation goes rampant?

While these concerns are legitimate, the answer to each is the same—you may need more funds in your investable asset bucket, and your finish line may become a little further out. However, there is still a finite number that is enough to meet your needs but also allows you to give generously and meet the needs of others.

In summary, you can factor any scenario into this analysis and project your unique, personalized, and changing net-worth curve. As you see that God is continuing to meet your needs, you can become more aggressive in your current giving rather than building a pile to give away through your will when your earthly sojourn is complete.

Returning to Roger and Alice from the beginning of the chapter, as I looked across the table at them, I asked, "What if I could show you that you will be okay? That given your current situation and the concerns you shared, there is a way to factor in all the variables and show you that you still have enough? That you can be generous with your wealth? Would you like to see it?" They both smiled and said, "Yes."

What about you? Do you know your finish line? Do you know how much you can potentially give away? Let me encourage you to look at your numbers and avoid the warning given in Ecclesiastes 5:13: "I have seen a grievous evil under the sun: wealth hoarded to the harm of its owners" (NIV). As discussed earlier in the chapter, John Wesley understood that to avoid this evil we need to invest in what matters for eternity by storing less for ourselves, finding our finish line, and giving more generously according to God's will.

CHAPTER 10

Estate Planning
and Foundations

Arthur and I were meeting to discuss some questions he had about his foundation, which he had set up many years earlier when he was still working and had a consistent income. Now Arthur was in his 80s, and the foundation had grown to over $20 million, which created some opportunities and dilemmas for him.

First, he was concerned that if he did not give the funds away during his lifetime, then his children might not give them in a manner he agreed with, such as to organizations inconsistent with his beliefs.

Second, Arthur realized that, given his age, he needed to give away several million dollars a year, which was much more than he had been giving, and he was not sure where to give it.

I have met with many people like Arthur over the years. They set up a foundation or make it part of their financial lives to gain a tax deduction and create a lasting legacy that links their family name with good works. However, they often do not think through the details of a foundation or clearly understand some of the potential unintended consequences.

In chapter 7 we talked about deferred giving—donations given through a will or estate plan. Put simply, there are three places your assets can go: your heirs, charity, or the IRS. An estate plan lays out who gets what and when. On the Beyond Estate Planning chart (Figure 10.1), you will note that the first question asks how much someone will leave to heirs and how much to charity.[26] The amount we leave to our heirs, including children, is a complex and nuanced question with many factors, like age, responsibility, spiritual maturity, etc. This decision requires a significant amount of prayer, reflection, and wisdom.

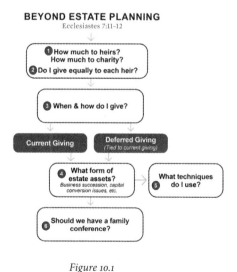

Figure 10.1

---

26   For more detailed explanations of the other questions in this chart, refer to
     Splitting Heirs by Ron Blue.

Estate tax laws allow us to leave a certain amount to our heirs without incurring an estate tax. A common estate planning technique is to leave this amount to our children and anything over this amount to a charitable entity (often through a foundation) to avoid all estate tax.[27] As we have discussed previously, we should give generously during our lifetime (current giving), but since we do not know when we will leave this earth, a foundation can be a tool to fund charities of our choice after our death.

What, Why, and When of a Foundation

Simply put, a charitable foundation is a tool that can provide many giving benefits. These include simplifying giving by donating from a central place, allowing for anonymous donations, enabling families to work together on generosity initiatives, and providing tax efficiencies in giving. You can set up a foundation during your lifetime or upon your death.

Let me illustrate how a foundation is simple to use. As we discussed previously, some people will need to consider their net worth to give as they have prospered. They may be able to give assets like business interests, closely held stock, land, real estate, publicly traded stocks, mutual funds, etc. However, many ministries are not set up to receive these non-cash gifts. By gifting these assets to a foundation, they can be liquidated and the cash funds allocated to multiple ministries of the donor's choice.

A foundation can also potentially provide tax efficiencies for current or deferred giving. Suppose you have an asset that has appreciated significantly over the years. Perhaps you paid $10 per share for a stock and now it is worth $100 per share. Instead of selling it, paying the capital gains tax of approximately $20 per share and reducing what you can give, you donate the stock to the foundation. As a charitable entity, when the foundation sells the stock, there is no capital gains tax due. So, when the foundation sells the shares, it

---

27　I am not recommending people leave the maximum amount possible to their children, but I have observed that this is often the choice people make.

has $100 per share for charity versus $80 per share if you had sold the stock on your own. This tax illustration is also true if you give straight to the ministry and bypass the foundation.

Foundation Options

When establishing a foundation, there are two options. One is a private foundation, and the other is a donor-advised fund (DAF). At the most basic level, the difference between the two options is how the entity is created and operates.

> *Private Foundation*: A wholly independent, tax-exempt legal entity governed by its own set of bylaws, articles of incorporation, etc.

> *Donor-Advised Fund (DAF)*: A giving account that is offered by and housed in a public charity, which may be connected to a community foundation, a financial institution, or a university.

These two charitable vehicles offer very different levels of control, authority, and philanthropic versatility.[28] Which option an individual chooses is determined by his or her goals. In my experience, most people with significant net worth should consider having a DAF for both their current giving and their deferred giving in their estate plan. If they decide to have a private foundation, then they should have both because of the tax advantages and anonymity offered by a DAF (review chapter 3 for the biblical principle of giving anonymously).

Unintended Consequences of a Foundation

If you decide to utilize a foundation during your lifetime or in your will to maximize your giving and train the next generation, it is important to recognize some potential unintended consequences.

---

28 For more details, consult a like-minded advisor who can further explain the differences and determine which option is best for you.

Funds stay put. After assets are transferred to a foundation, they often stay there indefinitely. You have already received the tax benefits and, as a result, may be in less of a hurry to gift the funds and put them to work for God's kingdom. This situation is where Arthur, from the beginning of the chapter, found himself. He had set up the foundation as a tool for giving to ministries, but over time he did not distribute funds at a rate that kept the foundation from growing. Now he had a compounded problem. Not only was the amount he needed to donate beyond his giving horizon because he did not have ministries in mind to give to, but he had also aged and had less time to distribute the funds during his lifetime.

Relegates stewardship responsibility to others. Death is inevitable, and you have to give your earthly wealth away at some point. You can't take it with you. So, if you leave assets in a foundation versus giving them to God's work during your lifetime, then they become the responsibility of your heirs to distribute. Unfortunately, you do not know if your heirs will use them for kingdom benefit, as Ecclesiastes 2:18–19 says: "I hated all my toil in which I toil under the sun, seeing that I must leave it to the man who will come after me, and who knows whether he will be wise or a fool? Yet he will be master of all for which I toiled and used my wisdom under the sun. This also is vanity." In relegating your responsibility to others, you have not leveraged your temporal goods for eternal gain.

Death is inevitable, and you have to give your earthly wealth away at some point.

A burden to heirs. The amount you leave for others to distribute can create a burden for them. They may worry that they won't gift it like you would have wanted, or they could give it in a way that goes against your values. They may feel frustrated by the responsibility that was left to them and wish you would have dealt with it before your death.[29]

A way to employ family members. Sometimes people keep a large foundation active to employ family members, which can enable them to skirt independent responsibility by not requiring them to find other employment. Unfortunately, when this becomes the purpose of the foundation, the funds usually do not get put to work for God's kingdom.

Ongoing management and maintenance costs. Keeping a foundation alive and current incurs investment management fees and ongoing administration costs. A private foundation is more expensive to maintain than a DAF, but both have perpetual costs. Therefore, make sure your foundation is serving a purpose and not just accumulating assets without a goal.

Lack of impact. If you want to convert temporal funds into eternal currency, then it is imperative to put your wealth to work. Your life carries influence, but most of that impact will remain unseen. At the end of the book *Middlemarch*, George Eliot speaks about the protagonist, Dorothea Brooke, a woman who invested in the lives of others and their needs and therefore never fully attained her potential. However, the last paragraph of the book says,

> But the effect of her being on those around her was incalculably diffusive: for the growing good of the world is partly dependent on unhistoric acts; and that things are not so ill with you and me as they might have been, is half owing to the number who lived faithfully a hidden life, and rest in unvisited tombs.[30]

29　During your lifetime, you can use a foundation to train the next generation in generosity and stewardship. Families working together to make grants from a family foundation or DAF can have valuable discussions, expand their giving options, and prepare heirs to have a generous mindset after the patriarch and matriarch are gone.

30　George Eliot, *Middlemarch* (Middlesex, UK: Penguin Books, 1965), 896.

The words "incalculably diffusive" can describe your impact as well, which is difficult to quantify, count, or measure. You most likely will not know the impact of your giving on others and the world around you on this side of heaven. However, you can know that if your assets are sitting in a foundation, then there is no incalculably diffusive impact from them, and they are not being used for God's kingdom work.

You most likely will not know the impact of your giving on others and the world around you on this side of heaven.

Mission drift or lack of flexibility. Sometimes those who inherit a foundation do not distribute the assets to further the same mission or purpose as the founder (which results in mission drift), or the founder's purpose for the funds is so specific and restrictive that the heirs cannot deploy them in a worthwhile manner.

I was at a meeting once in which we were discussing the funds someone had left in a foundation in the 1950s that were specifically designated for "upkeep and maintenance of the church." The foundation was governed by an irrevocable legal document that could not be changed to divert the funds for other uses. Now, seventy years later, the foundation has over $30 million in it, but this church does not have a need for that amount of upkeep and maintenance. It is virtually impossible to use even the earnings on the assets each year for upkeep and maintenance, so the $30 million sits in the foundation not being used in a worthwhile manner. The purpose of the foundation sounded good to the founder, but without thinking about the limited scope of that designation in the future, an unintended consequence occurred.

These are some of the challenges of creating institutional structures and using vehicles for giving, like foundations, versus aggressively giving now and investing that money in God's kingdom sooner. Remember the concept of reverse compounding from chapter 7? It applies here. Sometimes foundations end up existing just for the sake of existing, without being leveraged for kingdom gain.

Is there ever a place for a long-standing, ongoing foundation that does not distribute all of its assets but rather grows them in order to have long-term giving capacity? Given our discussion of rewards, reverse compounding, and unintended consequences of foundations, I would conclude that it is ill-advised to have an active, ongoing foundation or DAF after your death. It may exist for a short time while heirs disburse the funds, but it should have a *limited shelf life*. Every situation is different, but it's important to remember that the reason for our giving should be to honor God and obey His commands.

CONCLUSION

Putting the Principles into Practice

Kenneth Boa and Russ Crosson

Scripture teaches us to treat things according to their true value—this is the definition of biblical wisdom. When we accumulate earthbound wealth, we are treating what is temporal as if it were eternal. But God invites us to be rich toward Him by leveraging that which is passing away for eternal gain. Throughout this book, we've pointed you to the biblical principles of leveraging your wealth for God's kingdom and given you practical ways to do so. Now, it's time to apply the principles and practices to your own life.

As you seek to be obedient to God's commands and give your wealth away, remember that the more you understand God's extravagant generosity toward you, the more generous you will become. God sent His own Son to die on the cross for your sins, taking on His wrath and making a way for you to have eternal life in Him. Nothing could be more generous than that! We should not take a legalistic approach to generosity, giving out of a reluctant heart in order to try to earn God's favor. At the same time, we should not hold tightly to the things of this world, striving to find security in our wealth, because our true security is in our adoption as children of God. When we realize that nothing we do can make God love us more or less, we can see our accumulation of earthly treasure for what it really is: foolish, misguided, unproductive, and an obstacle to closeness with God.

How do we know if we have fallen into this foolishness? We're quick to identify fools in our lives, but we've never seen one in the mirror . . . right? We don't like being foolish, looking foolish, or being called foolish. Yet it is easy to forget the truth about who we are in Christ and invest our time, talent, and treasure in foolish things that have no value.

We thought it might be helpful to assemble some questions about finances based on biblical admonitions as a litmus test. Just as comedian Jeff Foxworthy asks the question, "You might be a redneck if . . .," we wanted to have the test, "You might be a fool if . . ." Answer "yes" or "no" to the following questions:

1. Do you regularly seek out the counsel and opinions of wise Christians in making decisions about your finances? Do you have like-minded advisors that share your values and worldview? (Proverbs 15:22)
2. Do you have an accountability partner for your finances? (Proverbs 18:1)
3. Are you guarding against greed and the love of money? (Hebrews 13:5)
4. Do you spend time in prayer seeking to know and follow God's will for your finances? (Proverbs 16:16; James 1:5)
5. Do you think before you spend and seek to honor God instead of satisfying yourself with money? (Proverbs 3:9; 13:11)
6. Do you invest your time wisely, focusing on building spiritual and social capital, not just financial capital? (Psalm 90:12; Proverbs 22:9)
7. Do you avoid get-rich-quick schemes? (Proverbs 20:21; 1 Timothy 6:6–12)

8. Are you spending less than you earn, getting out of debt, and giving generously toward those in need? (Proverbs 22:26–27; Romans 13:7–8)
9. When your "cup runneth over" (Psalm 23:5), do you avoid getting a bigger cup? (Luke 12:16–21; 2 Corinthians 9:6)
10. Is there concrete evidence in your bank account that you live in anticipation of Christ's return? (Matthew 25:1–13; 1 Thessalonians 5:1–11)

You might be a fool if you consistently answered "no" to the majority of these questions. When reviewing these questions, our natural tendency is to excuse our foolish behavior as an anomaly. However, foolishness is more a way of life than a single act. Ask God to open your eyes to areas of foolishness in your life. The good news is, He is faithful to supply wisdom when you ask (James 1:5)! You do not need to remain stagnant in your faith, but you can and should grow in all of these areas, even if you are already putting biblical principles into practice.

Another way to test yourself is with the following chart. Circle what best describes you in each row.

WISE	FOOL
Accountable	Not accountable
Gives according to ability	Gives what feels comfortable
Gives now (warm hand)	Gives later (cold hand)
Seeks wise counsel	Does not seek wise counsel
Meets others' needs	Ignores others' needs
Has a will	Does not have a will
Has good grasp of financial situation	Not sure of financial situation
Generous	Stingy

Here's the bottom line: a wise life is a generous life. In order to be truly generous, we need to live with eternity in sight.

Consider this: the first thing we do when we travel to a new country is convert one kind of currency into another because we know that our former bills and coins are useless in the new country. Similarly, if we believe in Jesus as our Lord and Savior, we need to exchange our earthly currency for heavenly currency. In its rightful place, money becomes a vehicle by which God's lavish love and extravagant provision are extended to His people, and by participating in this incredible kingdom work, each of us grows in our capacity to serve and trust our Creator. At the *bēma*, the judgment seat of Christ, God will hold us accountable for what we have done with the wealth entrusted to us. Our hope is that this book has given you some insights into how to leverage your prosperity for the kingdom of God. May God be with you and bless you as you seek to honor Him with your time, talent, and treasure.

Appendix

The following material, which was adapted from a Kingdom Advisors[31] resource, divides where to give into three main categories: the ministry of God's Word, the ministry of God's mercy, and the ministry of God's justice. It is further divided into the smaller categories of evangelism; preaching; teaching; discipleship; the poor and needy; prisoners; food, clothing, and shelter; healing and recovery; widows and orphans; the oppressed; and helpless victims. It is our hope that the verses included will aid you as you prayerfully evaluate a particular ministry or charity to which you are considering giving.

Ministry of God's Word

Matthew 28:18–20: And Jesus came up and spoke to them, saying, "All authority has been given to Me in heaven and on earth. Go therefore and make disciples of all the nations, baptizing them in the name of the Father and the Son and the Holy Spirit, teaching them to observe all that I commanded you; and lo, I am with you always, even to the end of the age."

Luke 11:28: "Blessed are those who hear the word of God and observe it."

Luke 24:46–47: He said to them, "Thus it is written, that the Christ would suffer and rise again from the dead the third day, and that repentance for forgiveness of sins would be proclaimed in His name to all the nations, beginning from Jerusalem."

---

31 See p. 158 for more information on Kingdom Advisors. All Scripture verses in this appendix are in the NASB 1995.

Acts 1:8: "But you will receive power when the Holy Spirit has come upon you; and you shall be My witnesses both in Jerusalem, and in all Judea and Samaria, and even to the remotest part of the earth."

Acts 4:31: And when they had prayed, the place where they had gathered together was shaken, and they were all filled with the Holy Spirit and began to speak the word of God with boldness.

Acts 6:7: The word of God kept on spreading; and the number of the disciples continued to increase greatly in Jerusalem, and a great many of the priests were becoming obedient to the faith.

Acts 12:24: But the word of the Lord continued to grow and to be multiplied.

Colossians 1:25: Of this church I was made a minister according to the stewardship from God bestowed on me for your benefit, so that I might fully carry out the preaching of the word of God.

Evangelism

Matthew 24:14: This gospel of the kingdom shall be preached in the whole world as a testimony to all the nations, and then the end will come.

Mark 16:15: And He said to them, "Go into all the world and preach the gospel to all creation."

Luke 4:43: But He said to them, "I must preach the kingdom of God to the other cities also, for I was sent for this purpose."

Luke 8:1: Soon afterwards, He began going around from one city and village to another, proclaiming and preaching the kingdom of God.

Acts 20:24: But I do not consider my life of any account as dear to myself, so that I may finish my course and the ministry which I received from the Lord Jesus, to testify solemnly of the gospel of the grace of God.

Romans 10:14: How then will they call on Him in whom they have not believed? How will they believe in Him whom they have not heard? And how will they hear without a preacher?

1 Corinthians 1:17: For Christ did not send me to baptize, but to preach the gospel, not in cleverness of speech, so that the cross of Christ would not be made void.

1 Corinthians 9:14: So also the Lord directed those who proclaim the gospel to get their living from the gospel.

Philippians 1:3–6: I thank my God in all my remembrance of you, always offering prayer with joy in my every prayer for you all, in view of your participation in the gospel from the first day until now. For I am confident of this very thing, that He who began a good work in you will perfect it until the day of Christ Jesus.

Preaching

Matthew 11:1: When Jesus had finished giving instructions to His twelve disciples, He departed from there to teach and preach in their cities.

Mark 1:38: He said to them, "Let us go somewhere else to the towns nearby, so that I may preach there also; for that is what I came for."

Mark 2:2: And many were gathered together, so that there was no longer room, not even near the door; and He was speaking the word to them.

Acts 8:4: Therefore, those who had been scattered went about preaching the word.

Acts 15:35: But Paul and Barnabas stayed in Antioch, teaching and preaching with many others also, the word of the Lord.

1 Timothy 4:13: Until I come, give attention to the public reading of Scripture, to exhortation and teaching.

1 Timothy 5:17: The elders who rule well are to be considered worthy of double honor, especially those who work hard at preaching and teaching.

2 Timothy 4:2: Preach the word; be ready in season and out of season; reprove, rebuke, exhort, with great patience and instruction.

Teaching

Deuteronomy 4:9: "Only give heed to yourself and keep your soul diligently, so that you do not forget the things which your eyes have seen and they do not depart from your heart all the days of your life; but make them known to your sons and your grandsons."

Deuteronomy 11:19: "You shall teach them to your sons, talking of them when you sit in your house and when you walk along the road and when you lie down and when you rise up."

Mark 1:21: They went into Capernaum; and immediately on the Sabbath He entered the synagogue and began to teach.

Mark 6:34: When Jesus went ashore, He saw a large crowd, and He felt compassion for them because they were like sheep without a shepherd; and He began to teach them many things.

Acts 2:42: They were continually devoting themselves to the apostles' teaching and to fellowship, to the breaking of bread and to prayer.

Acts 5:21a: Upon hearing this, they entered into the temple about daybreak and began to teach.

Acts 18:11: And he settled there a year and six months, teaching the word of God among them.

Galatians 6:6: The one who is taught the word is to share all good things with the one who teaches him.

Titus 2:1: But as for you, speak the things which are fitting for sound doctrine.

Discipleship

Matthew 16:24: Then Jesus said to His disciples, "If anyone wishes to come after Me, he must deny himself, and take up his cross and follow Me."

Matthew 28:18–20: And Jesus came up and spoke to them, saying, "All authority has been given to Me in heaven and on earth. Go therefore and make disciples of all the nations, baptizing them in the name of the Father and the Son and the Holy Spirit, teaching them to observe all that I commanded you; and lo, I am with you always, even to the end of the age."

1 Corinthians 11:1: Be imitators of me, just as I also am of Christ.

Ephesians 4:11–13: And He gave some as apostles, and some as prophets, and some as evangelists, and some as pastors and teachers, for the equipping of the saints for the work of service, to the building up of the body of Christ; until we all attain to the unity of the faith, and of the knowledge of the Son of God, to a mature man, to the measure of the stature which belongs to the fullness of Christ.

Colossians 1:28: We proclaim Him, admonishing every man and teaching every man with all wisdom, so that we may present every man complete in Christ.

2 Timothy 2:2: The things which you have heard from me in the presence of many witnesses, entrust these to faithful men who will be able to teach others also.

Hebrews 13:7: Remember those who led you, who spoke the word of God to you; and considering the result of their conduct, imitate their faith.

Ministry of God's Mercy

Psalm 6:9: The LORD has heard my supplication, the LORD receives my prayer.

Psalm 25:6: Remember, O LORD, Your compassion and Your lovingkindnesses, for they have been from of old.

Psalm 28:6: Blessed be the LORD, because He has heard the voice of my supplication.

Hosea 6:6: For I delight in loyalty rather than sacrifice, and in the knowledge of God rather than burnt offerings.

Micah 6:8: He has told you, O man, what is good; and what does the LORD require of you but to do justice, to love kindness, and to walk humbly with your God?

Matthew 25:34–40: "Then the King will say to those on His right, 'Come, you who are blessed of My Father, inherit the kingdom prepared for you from the foundation of the world. For I was hungry, and you gave Me something to eat; I was thirsty, and you gave Me something to drink; I was a stranger, and you invited Me in; naked, and you clothed Me; I was sick, and you visited Me; I was in prison, and you came to Me.' Then the righteous will answer Him, 'Lord, when did we see You hungry, and feed You, or thirsty, and give You something to drink? And when did we see You a stranger, and invite You in, or naked, and clothe You? When did we see You sick, or in prison, and come to You?' The King will answer and say to them, 'Truly I say to you, to the extent that you did it to one of these brothers of Mine, even the least of them, you did it to Me.'"

Luke 6:36: "Be merciful, just as your Father is merciful."

Luke 10:37: And he said, "The one who showed mercy toward him." Then Jesus said to him, "Go and do the same."

Romans 11:30–31: For just as you once were disobedient to God, but now have been shown mercy because of their disobedience, so these also now have been disobedient, that because of the mercy shown to you they also may now be shown mercy.

Poor and Needy

Deuteronomy 15:11: "For the poor will never cease to be in the land; therefore I command you, saying, 'You shall freely open your hand to your brother, to your needy and poor in your land.'"

Psalm 9:18: For the needy will not always be forgotten, nor the hope of the afflicted perish forever.

Psalm 12:5: "Because of the devastation of the afflicted, because of the groaning of the needy, now I will arise," says the Lord; "I will set him in the safety for which he longs."

Psalm 35:10: All my bones will say, "Lord, who is like You, who delivers the afflicted from him who is too strong for him, and the afflicted and the needy from him who robs him?"

Psalm 140:12: I know that the Lord will maintain the cause of the afflicted and justice for the poor.

Proverbs 14:31: He who oppresses the poor taunts his Maker, but he who is gracious to the needy honors Him.

Proverbs 19:17: One who is gracious to a poor man lends to the LORD, and He will repay him for his good deed.

Proverbs 31:9: Open your mouth, judge righteously, and defend the rights of the afflicted and needy.

Isaiah 41:17: "The afflicted and needy are seeking water, but there is none, and their tongue is parched with thirst; I, the LORD, will answer them Myself, as the God of Israel I will not forsake them."

Jeremiah 22:16: "He pled the cause of the afflicted and needy; then it was well. Is not that what it means to know Me?" declares the LORD.

Matthew 6:3–4: "But when you give to the poor, do not let your left hand know what your right hand is doing, so that your giving will be in secret; and your Father who sees what is done in secret will reward you."

Prisoners

Psalm 102:19–20: For He looked down from His holy height; from heaven the LORD gazed upon the earth, to hear the groaning of the prisoner, to set free those who were doomed to death.

Isaiah 42:6–7: "I am the LORD, I have called You in righteousness, I will also hold You by the hand and watch over You, and I will appoint You as a covenant to the people, as a light to the nations, to open blind eyes, to bring out prisoners from the dungeon and those who dwell in darkness from the prison."

Isaiah 51:14: "The exile will soon be set free, and will not die in the dungeon, nor will his bread be lacking."

Matthew 25:36: "I was in prison, and you came to Me."

Luke 4:18: "The Spirit of the LORD is upon Me, because He anointed Me to preach the gospel to the poor. He has sent Me to proclaim release to the captives, and recovery of sight to the blind, to set free those who are oppressed."

Hebrews 10:34: For you showed sympathy to the prisoners and accepted joyfully the seizure of your property, knowing that you have for yourselves a better possession and a lasting one.

Hebrews 13:3: Remember the prisoners, as though in prison with them, and those who are ill-treated, since you yourselves also are in the body.

Food, Clothing, and Shelter

Deuteronomy 10:18: "He executes justice for the orphan and the widow, and shows His love for the alien by giving him food and clothing."

Psalm 107:8–9: Let them give thanks to the LORD for His loving-kindness, and for His wonders to the sons of men! For He has satisfied the thirsty soul, and the hungry soul He has filled with what is good.

Isaiah 58:6–8: "Is this not the fast which I choose, to loosen the bonds of wickedness, to undo the bands of the yoke, and to let the oppressed go free and break every yoke? Is it not to divide your bread with the hungry and bring the homeless poor into the house; when you see the naked, to cover him; and not to hide yourself from your own flesh? Then your light will break out like the dawn, and your recovery will speedily spring forth; and your righteousness will go before you; the glory of the LORD will be your rear guard."

Ezekiel 18:16: "[He does not] oppress anyone, or retain a pledge, or commit robbery, but he gives his bread to the hungry and covers the naked with clothing."

Matthew 25:35–36: "For I was hungry, and you gave Me something to eat; I was thirsty, and you gave Me something to drink; I was a stranger, and you invited Me in; naked, and you clothed Me; I was sick, and you visited Me."

Romans 12:20: But if your enemy is hungry, feed him, and if he is thirsty, give him a drink; for in so doing you will heap burning coals on his head.

James 2:14–16: What use is it, my brethren, if someone says he has faith but he has no works? Can that faith save him? If a brother or sister is without clothing and in need of daily food, and one of you says to them, "Go in peace, be warmed and be filled," and yet you do not give them what is necessary for their body, what use is that?

Healing and Recovery

Psalm 22:24: For He has not despised nor abhorred the affliction of the afflicted; nor has He hidden His face from him; but when he cried to Him for help, He heard.

Matthew 4:24: The news about Him spread throughout all Syria; and they brought to Him all who were ill, those suffering with various diseases and pains, demoniacs, epileptics, paralytics; and He healed them.

Matthew 9:35: Jesus was going through all the cities and villages, teaching in their synagogues and proclaiming the gospel of the kingdom, and healing every kind of disease and every kind of sickness.

Matthew 14:14: When He went ashore, He saw a large crowd, and felt compassion for them and healed their sick.

Matthew 15:30: And large crowds came to Him, bringing with them those who were lame, crippled, blind, mute, and many others, and they laid them down at His feet; and He healed them.

Luke 9:1-2: And He called the twelve together, and gave them power and authority over all the demons and to heal diseases. And He sent them out to proclaim the kingdom of God and to perform healing.

Luke 9:11: But the crowds were aware of this and followed Him; and welcoming them, He began speaking to them about the kingdom of God and curing those who had need of healing.

2 Corinthians 1:3-4: Blessed be the God and Father of our Lord Jesus Christ, the Father of mercies and God of all comfort, who comforts us in all our affliction so that we will be able to comfort those who are in any affliction with the comfort with which we ourselves are comforted by God.

Ministry of God's Justice

Psalm 33:5: He loves righteousness and justice; the earth is full of the lovingkindness of the LORD.

Psalm 45:6: Your throne, O God, is forever and ever; a scepter of uprightness is the scepter of Your kingdom.

Psalm 72:2: May he judge Your people with righteousness and Your afflicted with justice.

Psalm 89:14: Righteousness and justice are the foundation of Your throne; lovingkindness and truth go before You.

Psalm 106:3: How blessed are those who keep justice, who practice righteousness at all times!

Psalm 111:7: The works of His hands are truth and justice; all His precepts are sure.

Proverbs 21:3: To do righteousness and justice is desired by the LORD more than sacrifice.

Isaiah 58:6: "Is this not the fast which I choose, to loosen the bonds of wickedness, to undo the bands of the yoke, and to let the oppressed go free and break every yoke?"

Widows and Orphans

Deuteronomy 10:18: "He executes justice for the orphan and the widow, and shows His love for the alien by giving him food and clothing."

Deuteronomy 24:17: "You shall not pervert the justice due an alien or an orphan, nor take a widow's garment in pledge."

Deuteronomy 27:19: "'Cursed is he who distorts the justice due an alien, orphan, and widow.' And all the people shall say, 'Amen.'"

Psalm 68:5: A father of the fatherless and a judge for the widows, is God in His holy habitation.

Psalm 82:3: Vindicate the weak and fatherless; do justice to the afflicted and destitute.

James 1:27: Pure and undefiled religion in the sight of our God and Father is this: to visit orphans and widows in their distress, and to keep oneself unstained by the world.

Oppressed

Psalm 72:14: He will rescue their life from oppression and violence, and their blood will be precious in his sight.

Psalm 102:17: He has regarded the prayer of the destitute and has not despised their prayer.

Psalm 103:6: The LORD performs righteous deeds and judgments for all who are oppressed.

Psalm 146:7b: The LORD sets the prisoners free.

Proverbs 31:8: Open your mouth for the mute, for the rights of all the unfortunate.

Isaiah 1:17: Learn to do good; seek justice, reprove the ruthless, defend the orphan, plead for the widow.

Helpless Victims

Psalm 10:12: Arise, O LORD; O God, lift up Your hand. Do not forget the afflicted.

Proverbs 28:15: Like a roaring lion and a rushing bear is a wicked ruler over a poor people.

Psalm 41:1: How blessed is he who considers the helpless; the LORD will deliver him in a day of trouble.

Psalm 72:13: He will have compassion on the poor and needy, and the lives of the needy he will save.

Psalm 82:4: Rescue the weak and the needy; deliver them out of the hand of the wicked.

Isaiah 40:29: He gives strength to the weary, and to him who lacks might He increases power.

Matthew 9:36: Seeing the people, He felt compassion for them, because they were distressed and dispirited like sheep without a shepherd.

Acts 20:35: "In everything I showed you that by working hard in this manner you must help the weak and remember the words of the Lord Jesus, that He Himself said, 'It is more blessed to give than to receive.'"

Acknowledgements

Kenneth Boa:

I have known Russ Crosson for many years, due to our collaboration with the National Christian Foundation, and our mutual friendship with Ron Blue. I have long appreciated his sagacity, and this opportunity to combine biblical principles from a theologian with practical wisdom from a practitioner has led to a new thing—an accessible hybrid of perspective and application.

Louisa Baker and I conducted several interviews about accessing and adapting my writings and teaching series, and this led to a viable, working manuscript. I'm thankful for her editorial skills and for her critical role in moving this book from desire to birth.

Katie Robinson then skillfully adapted more of my resources to enhance the material, and she capably edited Russ's manuscript as well. Her attention to every detail was superb to see, and *Leverage* is a far stronger book due to her excellent work.

I have long profited from a fruitful and creative association with Jenny Abel. Jenny and I coauthored *Recalibrate Your Life*, an IVP book that provides the broad context in which *Leverage* is a significant component. Her excellence in polishing this manuscript and her remarkable oversight of the transition from manuscript to print-ready book was a pleasure to watch.

Stephen Crotts and I have forged a creative artistic collaboration, and it was a joy to work with him on the conceptualization of the cover and interior art. Stephen and I concur on the need for beauty to be a central part of books designed to bring honor to the Wellspring of beauty, goodness, and truth.

Victoria Corish's remarkable work on *The Angel and the Voyager* led us to entrust her with the layout of *Leverage*. Her elegant use of space and design has greatly enhanced this book.

I also express my gratitude for my Trinity House Publishers associates, Al Van Horne, Levi Kilian, and George Durant, for their suggestions and implementation in the publication of this practical guidebook to transmuting the lead of what is passing to the gold of what will never fade.

Karen, my bride of the new creation, is the person who completes me in the purposes of God, and our synergistic union has contributed to everything of enduring value in my ministry.

To the triune architect and narrator of the greatest story ever told. *Soli Deo gloria.*

Russ Crosson:

The creation of this book was possible through the efforts of a myriad of contributors. First, I am grateful to Kenneth Boa for allowing me to co-labor with him on this project. His desire to attack this topic is commendable, and the idea to combine a theologian and a practitioner makes it unique in the marketplace.

Malissa Light's editorial prowess, ability with words, and countless rewrites of the manuscript have made it compelling for the reader. I am so grateful for her ability to make me sound better and ensure the message of the book is clear.

As with all books I have undertaken, I owe a debt of gratitude to my partners at Ronald Blue Trust. Nick Stonestreet, Brian Shepler, and the rest of the leadership team have led the firm with skill, professionalism, and grace while allowing me time to work on this project. The hundreds of advisors at Ronald Blue Trust have shared the concepts in this book time and time again, for which I am grateful. It is upon their shoulders that I stand.

Special thanks to John Dodd for his insights and wisdom on the topic of generosity. We are grateful for his comments, and his insights have enhanced our process.

My long-time assistant Bonnie Davidson protected my calendar so I could write and effortlessly handled my many other demands on her time as this manuscript came together. This book would not have come to fruition without her contribution.

I am also always grateful for my wife, Julie. She was the first to challenge me with the concept of generosity, and her unwavering support and encouragement throughout the years have allowed me to implement the concepts shared in this book.

Finally, I am grateful that God (the greatest Giver) gave His Son Jesus Christ to die on the cross for my sins. Without God giving us both the incarnate Word (Jesus) and the written Word (the Bible), we would have no content for this book, and you would not have it in your hands.

About the Authors

Kenneth Boa

Kenneth Boa is engaged in a ministry of relational evangelism, discipleship, teaching, writing, and speaking. He holds a BS from Case Institute of Technology, a ThM from Dallas Theological Seminary, a PhD from New York University, and a DPhil from the University of Oxford in England.

Ken is the president and founder of Trinity House Publishers, Reflections Ministries, and Omnibus Media Ministries. Trinity House is dedicated to publishing materials that help people manifest eternal values in a temporal arena. Reflections seeks to encourage, teach, and equip people to know Christ, follow Him, become progressively conformed to His image, and reproduce His life in others. The mission of Omnibus Media is to generate transformative media to encourage global audiences to think, live, and act as they really are in Christ.

Ken's more than seventy books and publications include *Recalibrate Your Life*, *Shaped by Suffering*, *Life in the Presence of God*, *Rewriting Your Broken Story*, *Conformed to His Image*, *Faith Has Its Reasons*, *20 Compelling Evidences that God Exists*, and *Augustine to Freud*. He is a consulting editor of the *Zondervan NASB Study Bible* and has been a contributing editor for multiple other Bibles. He writes a free monthly teaching letter called *Reflections*; you can sign up to receive it and other resources at reflections.org.

Russ Crosson

Russ Crosson is executive vice president and chief mission officer of Ronald Blue Trust. Russ serves as chief advocate for the heart and soul of the organization and works to ensure the mission of the company is carried out with integrity in every area of the organization with a focus on making sure the company's mission is passed down and inculcated into future generations. Prior to his current position, Russ served as president and CEO of Ronald Blue & Co. from 2002 to 2017. He was hired by Ron Blue in 1980 as the second employee of Ronald Blue & Co.

Russ has worked extensively in all areas of financial planning, specializing in comprehensive financial, estate, and philanthropic planning, as well as generational family wealth management and transfer. From 1999 to 2002, Russ served as executive director of the National Christian Foundation. He graduated from Kansas State University with a BS in mathematics and a master's degree in education. Russ is the author of several books, including *Your Life . . . Well Spent, The Truth About Money Lies, What Makes a Leader Great,* and *Your Money Made Simple.* He has also been a featured speaker in many venues, including Promise Keepers, Issachar Summit, and America's Best Hope.

RonaldBlueTrust®
Wisdom for Wealth. *For Life.*

With nationwide capabilities, Ronald Blue Trust provides wealth management strategies and trust services based on biblical principles to help clients make wise financial decisions, live generously, and leave a lasting legacy. Through a network of branch offices, the company serves clients in all fifty states and offers services across the wealth spectrum in these key areas:

- Financial, retirement, and estate planning
- Investment management and solutions
- Charitable giving strategies
- Personal trust and estate settlement services
- Family office services
- Business consulting services
- Institutional investment management

Ronald Blue Trust offers many resources on the topics of financial planning, giving, family and life, economy and investments, leadership, and retirement. Please visit www.ronblue.com to view videos and newsletters in the company's Library, subscribe to its Insights blog, and learn more about its services.

www.ronblue.com | 800-841-0362 | info@ronblue.com

Kingdom Advisors ◀◀

More and more Christians are discovering the worldview of their financial advisor is of critical importance. Kingdom Advisors provides advocacy, training, and community for financial professionals who specialize in offering biblically wise advice. The group also offers distinction to its advisors by granting the Certified Kingdom Advisor designation, which provides a principled class of Christian financial advisors who have been trained in biblically wise financial advice.

Use Kingdom Advisors' "Find a Professional" directory search at kingdomadvisors.com to locate financial professionals who have demonstrated professional competence and a commitment to biblically wise financial counsel.

kingdomadvisors.com | 404-497-7680

Other Trinity House Publications

Kenneth Boa's handbook series:

Handbook to Prayer

Handbook to Renewal

Handbook to Scripture

Handbook to Leadership

Handbook to Wisdom

Simple Prayers

Handbook to Spiritual Growth

Handbook to God's Promises

Scripture Prayer Guide

Also from Trinity House:

Jesus in His Own Words

A Guide to Practicing God's Presence

A Journal of Sacred Readings

Purchase, or register to purchase and distribute, other Trinity House Publishers products at trinityhousepublishers.org.